CW01654344

To Proclaim Afresh

To Proclaim Afresh

Evangelical Agenda for the Church

Edited by Gordon Kuhrt

SPCK

First published in Great Britain 1995
Society for Promoting Christian Knowledge
Holy Trinity Church
Marylebone Road
London NW1 4DU

© The Contributors 1995

All rights reserved. No part of this book may be reproduced or transmitted in any form or by any means, electronic or mechanical, including photocopying, recording, or by any information storage and retrieval system, without permission in writing from the publisher.

Bible quotations are taken from the *New International Version*, copyright © 1973, 1978, 1984 by the International Bible Society. Published by Hodder & Stoughton (pages 12–13) and from the *New Revised Standard Version* © 1989 the Division of Education of the National Council of the Churches of Christ in the USA (page 75).

British Library Cataloguing-in-Publication Data
A catalogue record for this book is available from the British Library

ISBN 0-281-04905-X

Typeset by David Gregson Associates, Beccles, Suffolk
Printed in Great Britain by
Biddles Ltd., Guildford and King's Lynn

CONTENTS

The Contributors

MICHAEL BAUGHEN is Bishop of Chester. The editor of numerous songbooks, including *Youth Praise* and *Psalm Praise*, he is co-author (with Myrtle Baughen) of *Your Marriage* (Hodder 1994) and author of *The Prayer Principle* (Candle 1995).

CHRISTINA BAXTER is Dean of St John's College Nottingham, and Vice-Chairman of the House of Laity of the General Synod of the Church of England. She is the editor of *Stepping Stones: Joint Essays on Anglican Catholic and Evangelical Unity* (Hodder 1987).

GORDON BRIDGER is Principal of Oak Hill Theological College, London.

GEORGE CAREY is Archbishop of Canterbury. His most recent publications include *I Believe* (SPCK 1991) and *Sharing a Vision* (DLT 1993).

GRAHAM CRAY is Principal of Ridley Hall, Cambridge, and author of *The Gospel and Tomorrow's Culture* (CPAS 1994).

DICK FRANCE is Principal of Wycliffe Hall, Oxford, and an Honorary Canon of Ibadan Cathedral. His most recent publications include *Divine Government* (SPCK 1990), *Evangelical Anglicans* (co-edited with Alister McGrath)

(SPCK 1993), and *Women in the Church's Ministry* (Paternoster 1995).

PHILIP HACKING is Vicar of Fulwood, Sheffield, and Chairman of *Reform.* He is the author of *Free to Serve and Free to Suffer* (Crossway 1994).

GORDON KUHRT is Archdeacon of Lewisham. He is the author of *Believing in Baptism* (Mowbray 1987), and editor of *Doctrine Matters* (Hodder 1993).

SANDY MILLAR is Vicar of Holy Trinity, Brompton.

MICHAEL NAZIR-ALI is Bishop of Rochester. Formerly General Secretary of CMS, he is the author of *Islam: A Christian Perspective* (Paternoster 1983), *Frontiers in Muslim/Christian Encounter* (Regnum 1987), *From Everywhere to Everywhere* (Collins 1991), and *Mission and Dialogue* (SPCK 1995).

GAVIN REID is Bishop of Maidstone. His most recent publications include *To Reach a Nation* (Hodder 1987), *Our Place in His Story* (BRF), and (with Shelagh Brown) *Brushing up on Believing* (BRF).

MICHAEL TURNBULL is Bishop of Durham and Chairman of the Archbishops' Commission on the Organisation of the Church of England.

Publisher's Note

Apart from the Editor's Introduction, the chapters in this book are based on the addresses given at the Evangelical Anglican Leaders' Conference held in January 1995. All contributions have been revised and edited, and in many cases substantially expanded, although the original spoken style of the addresses has largely been retained. Chapter four draws on material prepared for the Archbishops' Commission on the Organisation of the Church of England, which is reproduced by permission of the Central Board of Finance of the Church of England.

Each writer wishes to emphasize that they accept responsibility *only* for their own contributions.

We are grateful to Dr Richard Burridge, Dean of King's College London, for his help and advice in facilitating the publication of this book.

Introduction

The present agenda will always be affected by our history and should be directed to the future. The genesis of the Evangelical Anglican Leaders' Conference needs to be understood in its historical context, and in the light of the dynamics of the growth of the Evangelical movement.

1950s–1990s

The first half of the twentieth century was generally a period of weakness and lack of confidence for the evangelical movement in the Church of England. At the close of the nineteenth century it was strong in numbers but weak in intellect and leadership. Evangelicals found it difficult to give coherent and convincing responses to the developments arising from the 'catholic' Oxford Movement which started in the 1830s, and to the liberal ideas linked to Darwin and biblical criticism. In addition they were torn with internal dissension in the 1920s and 30s, and seen to be essentially negative and reactionary about reform of the Prayer Book. Increasingly becoming a minority amongst the clergy, the signs of defensive paranoia developed. Though individual parishes showed spiritual life, evangelistic concern and missionary fervour, there was widespread suspicion about the Church at large and its bishops, about scholarship, theology, culture and social issues.

Signs of a change could be noted in the 1950s. Before the Second World War public school boys were being brought to faith and nurtured in Bible teaching and leadership through summer camps. In 1938 the Inter-Varsity Fellowship of University Christian Unions created its Biblical Research Committee. Crusader Bible Classes were influential. In 1945 John Stott was ordained curate at All Souls', Langham Place and five years later became Rector. In the 1950s and 60s he remarkably initiated, inspired and co-ordinated a series of enterprises which led to significant increase in strength and confidence. These included the life of his parish, his University Missions, his refounding of the Eclectic Society for younger evangelical clergy, his lectures, writings and encouragement of scholarship and publications, and his founding of and influence on the Church of England Evangelical Council and its international network, the Evangelical Fellowship of the Anglican Communion. All these factors and the visits of Dr Billy Graham led to a significant increase in evangelical ordinands. There was a knock-on effect on the evangelical theological colleges, youth work (especially Pathfinders), and the liveliness and fresh thinking in many parishes.

The recovery became publicly focused in the National Evangelical Anglican Congress at Keele University in 1967 when one thousand delegates hammered out an Agreed Statement. John Stott summarized succinctly his view of the three major residential NEACs of 1967, 1977 and 1988:

> NEAC 1 (Keele 1967) reflected on the church's message, mission, relation to the world, structures, worship and unity. Yet I think it fair to identify its dominant theme as *Involvement.* We resolved to take our place responsibly in the visible church and the secular world, and repented of our pietistic withdrawal from both.

> NEAC 2 (Nottingham 1977) had an even fuller agenda. *The Nottingham Statement* contained 20 sections on a wide variety of topics and 12 'Declarations of Intent'. Yet what caught people's attention and permeated every debate was *Hermeneutics*, the process of understanding the Bible. We resolved in future to listen to Scripture with conscientious care and integrity, and we repented of the naive, selective and even manipulative use of Scripture, of which we had sometimes been guilty. Whether we have kept our resolve is another matter.
>
> At NEAC 3 (Caister 1988) a great many issues were raised, particularly in the 70 or so workshops. Yet I am wondering if the dominant theme may prove to be *Integration*, or the bringing together of bits and pieces into a single whole. Because of the fall we are all disintegrated personalities; in Christ we are becoming re-integrated. We heard appeals to repent of our partial responses to Jesus Christ and of our subtle compromises with the world. We also heard several expressions of resolve to integrate the different departments of our lives, especially our beliefs and our behaviour, and our different callings in the church, under the supreme lordship of Jesus.[1]

The Keele Congress was the first and smallest but the most significant. It has been widely described as a turning point or watershed.[2] An observer, Canon D. M. Paton, Secretary of the Missionary and Ecumenical Council of the Church Assembly, commented

> First, the generally positive and open attitude of the congress confirmed the change of temper among Evangelicals which has been noticeable for some years in theological writing, ecumenical work, overseas mission and social ethics.
>
> Second, this change is not in the body of evangelical doctrine, but in the way the doctrines are held

and in the readiness to tackle new questions. In this respect, Keele seemed not unlike Vatican II!

Thirdly, a question. Have Evangelicals fully grasped that to play a real part in the corporate life of the Church of England involves taking very seriously (positively as well as negatively) the existence and views of those in the Church of England who are not Conservative Evangelicals? [3]

In his report of NEAC 3 (1988), John Stott spoke of five major commitments:

- to *theology* – which is integrated into action
- to *Scripture* – with which is integrated proper interpretation and an understanding of cultural contexts.
- to *mission* – in which is integrated evangelism and social responsibility, power and weakness.
- to the *Church* – which is integrated with a concern for its continual reformation, unity and truth.
- to *spirituality* – with the integration of the personal, moral, emotional and social dimensions.[4]

If you were to ask me how evangelicals have worked on these commitments, I would have to reply – *patchily.* If asked how evangelicals have worked towards integration (the bringing together of bits and pieces into a single whole), I can only reply – *uneasily.* There are numerous superb and encouraging developments, but there are unhelpful and disturbing trends as well. An appropriate analysis of these requires some understanding of:

The Dynamics of Growth

The evangelical movement has grown very significantly in the Church of England in the second half of the twentieth century. However, that movement is part of a much wider development that is both inter-denominational and international. Evangelicals have been increasingly influential within Anglicanism and upon world Christianity, but the influences have, of course, not been only one way. Evangelicals have increasingly left the ghetto and sectarian mentality, and have mixed, prayed, studied and shared in mission with Christians of many traditions. This mutual, two-way influencing results in complex interrelationships. It means that simple stereotypes and black-and-white judgements about evangelical orthodoxy and soundness are increasingly superficial and misleading.

Before we look at some examples of this two-way influence, we note that several wider movements have related to the revival of evangelicalism. The work of Karl Barth and the biblical theology movement have weakened the confidence of classical liberal theology and biblical criticism. The Roman Catholic renewal movements, the Second Vatican Council and the liturgical movement have brought renewed emphasis on Scripture, simplicity and congregational participation. The charismatic renewal movements have added their emphases on personal experience of spiritual reality, joyful witness and the spiritual gifts given to all God's people. The influence of African and South American Christians emphasizes the priority of evangelism, and need for structural flexibility. All these have assisted in different ways the evangelical resurgence.

A very clear example of the complexities of multilateral influence is in the area of spirituality. Evangelical spirituality has traditionally emphasized conversion, assurance of salvation, the cross, personal holiness, Scripture and active service.[5]

These emphases have been increasingly influential in other traditions. But many evangelicals have learned from others to value in a new way spiritual direction, retreat, the daily offices (and even Eucharist), the liturgical year, colour, symbolism and movement and a generally more sacramental ethos! This *can* lead to a weakened grasp of biblical elements in the evangelical traditions, but it is not inevitably so.[6]

Further examples could be developed in liturgy, use of the Bible, theological scholarship, ethics, mission, diocesan leadership and in General Synod.

Thus one of the growing tensions among evangelicals (both within the Church of England and beyond) is whether being receptive to influences of other theological and church traditions is an openness to the Spirit, or compromise with error. However, the evangelical (and Anglican) test is to ask whether the influence is scriptural, consonant with Scripture or, at the very least, not contrary to Scripture.

It is a commonplace to note that the growth of almost any movement leads to a broadening and diversification of interests and concerns. Edges and boundaries lose their sharpness. Some may lose their way in the broad spaces of new freedoms; others may react back into sectarian, narrow and rigid 'certainties' of a previous generation.[7]

The Genesis of the EALC

Charismatic and renewal groups have their own literature, organizations and conferences. The Reform Group which emerged among conservative evangelicals dismayed by the General Synod's decision for women priests has its conferences too. There are other evangelical special interest groups which plan conferences – in the Church of England there are Eclectics, SEACC (Senior Evangelical Anglican Clergy Conference), Church Society and many others. In the wider evangelical world there is Spring Harvest, Keswick Convention, Proclamation Trust, Tyndale Fellowship study groups etc., etc. The annual Anglican Evangelical Assembly which has met since 1983 is designed to be a relatively small 'delegate' assembly. So it could be argued that there was a vacuum because of the lack of an umbrella conference for the broad spread of evangelical Anglicans.

Canon Michael Saward invited several colleagues to meet on 30 March 1994 to discuss some of these matters, and we agreed to organize a conference in January 1995. The initial participants were the Bishops of Chester (Michael Baughen) and Southwark (Roy Williamson), Bishop Michael Nazir-Ali (then General Secretary of the Church Missionary Society), the Dean of Peterborough (Michael Bunker), Canon John Moore (General Secretary of the Church Pastoral-Aid Society) Canon Michael Saward (of St Paul's Cathedral) and the Archdeacon of Lewisham (Gordon Kuhrt). We immediately invited the Bishop of Maidstone (Gavin Reid) and Mrs Jill Dann (former Vice-Chairman of the House of Laity of General Synod) to join us and this group became the Organizing Committee with the Bishop of Chester as Chairman and Archdeacon Kuhrt as Secretary.

Early objectives were to focus evangelical leadership, to address vital issues, to provide a platform for bishops, theologians and strategists and perhaps to fill the vacuum that seems to have developed after the demise of the annual Islington Clerical Conference.

The Conference brochure was inserted in every copy of the *Church Times* and *Church of England Newspaper* in September 1994. The leaflet included these paragraphs:

> The programme will attempt to cover various issues concerning the Church, the evangelisation of our nation, and at the heart of all, Jesus, the Son of God. Those participating may represent different emphases within the Evangelical movement but all are united in wishing 'to proclaim afresh' the 'faith uniquely revealed in the Holy Scriptures and set forth in the Catholic Creeds'. The Conference is not intended to be confrontational, nor a 'point-scoring' exercise, nor even a 'peace-making' event. It will aim to stimulate Evangelical thinking as we approach the new century.

> The Evangelical movement in the Church of England is going through convulsive times and many have urged those bishops known as Evangelicals to give a clear lead. More than 20 bishops expect to be present and a group of them have sponsored the Conference to show how seriously they take that responsibility.

The Bishop of Chester wrote in the brochure:

> Today's Evangelicals in the Church of England face tremendous opportunities and challenges. At such a moment in history we need to strengthen and encourage one another, to think, to learn, and to plan strategies together.
>
> So, your episcopal brothers-in-Christ have set up this special Conference to provide a meeting point for Evangelicals in leadership at all levels. We have invited speakers (and respondents) who will address the issues facing us, with particular focus on the Church, its mission to our nation, and on the key doctrine of the Person of our Lord Jesus, now increasingly under attack.

The Conference title 'to proclaim afresh' comes from the Preface to the Declaration of Assent in the Ordinal

> The Church of England is part of the one, holy, catholic, and apostolic Church ... It professes the faith uniquely revealed in the holy Scriptures and set forth in the catholic creeds, which faith the Church is called upon to proclaim afresh in each generation.[8]

For the venue, the Committee made initial enquiries to Church House, Westminster and to some large City churches. Finally they fixed on the City Temple, Holborn, which could seat about 900. However, within three weeks the Conference was fully booked and applications continued to pour in. On 20 October, the venue was changed to Westminster Chapel which takes twice as many. This was not ideal because smaller ancillary halls were not available at such short notice, but over 1500 eventually booked.

This book contains the addresses delivered at the Conference, but some contributions have been extensively augmented.

Looking Ahead

Over half of those who attended returned a Response Form. Of those, 85 per cent wanted a similar conference next year. The major issues they wished to be addressed were the interpretation and authority of the Bible, and the complex of issues about evangelism, culture and apologetics.

In the light of these clear indications, there is planned a further Evangelical Anglican Leaders' Conference on 5 and 6 January 1996 at Westminster Central Hall.

Notes

1. J. R. W. Stott, '*What is the Spirit saying ... ?' A Report on NEAC 3* (Church of England Evangelical Council, 1988), p. 3.
2. See, e.g. Adrian Hastings, *A History of English Christianity 1920–1985* (London, Collins, 1986), pp. 553f.
3. In Philip Crowe (ed.), *Keele '67* (London, Falcon Books, CPAS, 1967), p. 16.
4. Stott, '*What is the Spirit Saying ... ?*', pp. 3–12.
5. See, e.g. David K. Gillett, *Trust and Obey – Explorations in Evangelical Spirituality* (London, Darton, Longman & Todd, 1993).
6. See the Grove Booklets on Spirituality (Bramcote, Notts., Grove Books).
7. See books under Further Reading.
8. Alternative Service Book, p. 387.

Further Reading

For the history:

G. R. Balleine, *A History of the Evangelical Party* (London, 1908).

D. W. Bebbington, *Evangelicalism in Modern Britain: a History from the 1730s to the 1980s* (London, Unwin Hyman, 1989).

K. Hylson-Smith, *Evangelicals in the Church of England 1734–1984* (Edinburgh, T & T Clark, 1989).

R. Manwaring, *From Controversy to Coexistence: Evangelicals in the Church of England 1914–1980* (Cambridge, Cambridge University Press, 1985).

Michael Saward, *The Anglican Church Today: Evangelicals on the Move* (Mowbrays, London, 1987).

For the conferences:

1967 J. I. Packer (ed.), *Guidelines – Anglican Evangelicals Face the Future* (London, Falcon Books, 1967); P. Crowe, *Keele '67 – the National Evangelical Anglican Congress Statement* (London, Falcon Books, 1967).

1977 J. R. W. Stott (ed.), *Obeying Christ in a Changing World*, Vol. I *The Lord Christ*; Vol. II *The People of God*; Vol. III *The Changing World* (London, Collins, 1977); *The Nottingham Statement* (London, Falcon Books, 1977).

1988 J. R. W. Stott, *What is the Spirit Saying . . . ? A Report on NEAC 3* (Church of England Evangelical Council, 1988); P. Williams, 'NEAC 3: Retrospect and Prospect', *Anvil*, Vol. 5 (1988), No. 1, pp. 53–70.

See also:

C. Baxter (ed.), *Stepping Stones: Joint Essays on Anglican Catholic and Evangelical Unity* (London, Hodder & Stoughton, 1987).

C. O. Buchanan 'Anglican Evangelicalism: The State of the "Party"', *Anvil*, Vol. 1 (1984), No. 1, pp. 7–18;

'Evangelicalism: The Latest State of the Party', *Anvil*, Vol. 11 (1994), No. 2, pp. 103–110.

D. L. Edwards with J. Stott, *Essentials: A Liberal-Evangelical Dialogue* (London, Hodder & Stoughton, 1988).

R. T. France and A. E. McGrath, *Evangelical Anglicans: Their Role and Influence in the Church Today* (London, SPCK, 1993).

J. C. King (ed.) *Evangelicals Today: 13 Stock-taking Essays* (London, Lutterworth Press, 1973).

G. W. Kuhrt *Doctrine Matters* (London, Hodder, 1993).

A. McGrath, *Evangelicalism and the Future of Christianity* (Hodder & Stoughton, 1993);
The Renewal of Anglicanism (London, SPCK, 1993).

J. I. Packer, *The Evangelical Anglican Identity Problem: An Analysis* (Oxford, Latimer House, 1978).

G. Reid (ed.), *Hope for the Church of England?* (Kingsway Publications, 1986).

D. J. Tidball, *Who are the Evangelicals? Tracing the Roots of Today's Movements* (London, Marshall Pickering, 1994).

M. Tinker (ed.), *Restoring the Vision: Anglican Evangelicals Speak Out* (Eastbourne, MARC, 1990).

P. Williams, 'Forward From Basics: A Future for the Church of England?', *Anvil*, Vol. 12 (1995), No. 1, pp. 7–20.

N. T. Wright, *Evangelical Anglican Identity: the Connections between Bible, Gospel and Church* (Oxford, Latimer House, 1980).

CHAPTER ONE

The Sovereign Lord

An Exposition of Acts 4.23–31

Gordon Bridger

23 On their release, Peter and John went back to their own
people and reported all that the chief priests and elders
had said to them. 24 When they heard this they raised their
voices together in prayer to God. 'Sovereign Lord' they
said, 'you made the heaven and the earth and the sea and
everything in them. 25 You spoke by the Holy Spirit
through the mouth of your servant, our father David:
"Why do the nations rage and the peoples plot in vain?
26 The kings of the earth take their stand and the rulers
gather together against the Lord and against his
Anointed One."

27 Indeed Herod and Pontius Pilate met together with
the Gentiles and the people of Israel in this city to conspire
against your holy servant Jesus whom you anointed.
28 They did what your power and will had decided before-
hand should happen. 29 Now, Lord, consider their threats
and enable your servants to speak your word with great
boldness. 30 Stretch out your hand to heal and perform
miraculous signs and wonders through the name of your

> *holy servant Jesus.'* [31] *After they prayed, the place where they were meeting was shaken. And they were all filled with the Holy Spirit and spoke the word of God boldly. (NIV)*

I was in Tanzania a week before Christmas at the consecration of Hilkiah Omindo, the new Bishop of Mara. Hilkiah is studying at Oak Hill College this year, and I am tempted to say that he is typical of the high calibre of student at Oak Hill. I have fallen for that temptation! One of the bonuses of my visit was to fly in three of the planes belonging to the Missionary Aviation Fellowship. One was a frail looking six-seater. The engine took a bit of starting. The person next to me unhelpfully murmured 'even if the engine fails, these planes glide very well!' I began to feel a slight sense of panic. Then the pilot said, 'we always like to pray before we take off, so let's do that'. He added, 'when I say that, when there is an unbeliever on the plane, he usually goes into shock! But for you it will be different'. And it was. Focusing on God, praying to God, put everything in perspective again. I began to look forward to the flight – and it was terrific!

Now in Acts Chapter 4, something like that is happening. The growing Christian movement suddenly began to face opposition and difficulty. First by opposition from Jewish religious leaders, later of course by moral compromise and false teaching. Like us, they lived in convulsive times.

In Acts 4, Peter and John are forbidden to preach or teach at all in the name of Jesus. In Chapter 4, v. 12, they preach that uncompromising and uncomfortable truth about the uniqueness of Jesus.[1] 'Salvation is found in no-one else; for there is no other name under heaven given to men by which we must be saved.' The religious leaders could not take that, so they released them from prison but forbade them to preach that message. And when Peter and John reported this to the Christians there was probably a moment of panic. Then they focused on God, and their problems and their priorities were seen in a new perspective.

I believe that my task, in this Bible exposition, is to help us focus, not on our different agendas, but on God himself, the Sovereign Lord. This prayer, in Acts 4, will help us.

Notice, first, that these Christians pray to the 'Sovereign Lord of Creation'. 'Sovereign Lord' they pray. The word they use is one used of a slave owner, and a ruler of unchallengeable power, but here of One far greater than any human ruler. 'You made the heaven and the earth and the sea and everything in them.' In other words, they believed that God is the Creator and sustainer of the whole universe, and therefore could sustain them when under threat and pressure. Is that not exactly the message the prophet Isaiah had given to the Israelites when they were in exile?

> Why do you complain O Israel, 'My way is hidden from the Lord, my cause is disregarded by my God.' Do you not know? Have you not heard? The Lord is the everlasting God, the Creator of the ends of the earth. He will not grow tired or weary. He gives strength to the weary and increases the power of the weak. Even youths grow tired and weary, and young men stumble and fall; but those who hope in the Lord will renew their strength. They will soar on wings like eagles; they will run and not grow weary, they will walk and not faint. (Isa. 40.27–31)

As evangelicals we glory in the God of redemption; but let us not forget the God of creation. He who made and sustains the whole universe is well able to sustain you and me, however weary, or discouraged in our ministry we may be. God is the Sovereign Lord of creation, and will sustain and refresh us in our discipleship and ministries as we focus on him.

But notice, secondly, that they pray to the Sovereign Lord of Revelation (v. 25). That is, they not only believe that God made the world, they believe that God spoke by the Holy Spirit through the mouth of his servants, through the Scriptures: 'You Lord spoke by the Holy Spirit through the mouth of your servant, our father David.' And they quote Psalm 2, and make it clear that they believe that what the Scripture said, God said: 'YOU spoke (Lord) ... by the mouth of your servant, David.'

In other words the early Christians believed that the words that God had spoken to David to assure him that God was on his throne, and that he would not allow David's enemies to frustrate his plans, were words that equally applied to the early Church. God was speaking to the Christians of the first century, through the words of Scripture written centuries earlier.

Christians today can be encouraged in the same way through the Scriptures. We need not be afraid of human rulers, or anyone else who threatens us or opposes the work of God's 'Anointed One', Jesus (see v. 25).

So, as these Christians prayed, they showed they believed that *what Scripture says – God says.*[2] Is that not the classical Evangelical view of Scripture? the same view that Jesus held of the Old Testament Scriptures? Is it not the historic view of the Church of England? So let us focus on the God of revelation. We should expect him to speak to us through his word by his Spirit. We should test 'spiritual experiences' and spiritual phenomena by the Scriptures. We should search the Scriptures diligently together.

At Nottingham in 1977, at the NEAC Conference, John Stott said this:

> 'We evangelicals are Bible people. We believe that God has spoken fully and finally in His Son Jesus Christ, and in the biblical witness to Christ. We believe that Scripture is precisely the written speech of God, and that because it is God's Word it has

> supreme authority over the Church. The supremacy of Scripture has always been, and always will be, the first hallmark of an Evangelical.'

A little later he went on to say, 'we see it as part of our evangelical responsibility to remind our Church of its official stance and to seek by prayer, argument, and example, to bring it back to its lost moorings.'[3] We have the same task today. For God is the Sovereign God, not only of creation but revelation.

These Christians also prayed to the Sovereign Lord of history. They focused on that day in history – the day that changed the world – when Jesus died for our sins, and finished the work of salvation God had given him to do. From one point of view, of course, the death of Christ looks like a tragedy: 'Herod and Pontius Pilate met together to conspire against your holy servant Jesus, whom you anointed', they prayed; and it looked as if evil had triumphed. But they knew, in the light of the resurrection, that God is Sovereign in history. God was working his purposes out through the cross. The God who is the God of history, is also the God of Calvary. And it was at the cross that they found not only forgiveness and peace with God, but hope. Look again at v. 28: 'They did what your power and will had decided beforehand should happen.' God was working his purposes out, through suffering and weakness and sacrifice in the midst of a sinful and rebellious world. God was working all things according to the counsel of his will (see Eph. 1.11).

So as we focus on the Sovereign Lord of history, let's look to the cross of Jesus. I do not know whether you ever feel like despairing at the increasing inroads of secularism on our society, or maybe at the Church of England itself. If you do, look to the God of Calvary, look to the cross, and you will find hope, as well as forgiveness! For God is the Sovereign Lord of history.

And surely it was because they focused on the Sovereign

God of creation, revelation and history, that they were able to pray as they did? 'Now Lord, consider their threats' (v. 29). Their problems were seen in a new perspective. In fact they did not spend a lot of time looking at their difficulties or problems! Rather they went on, 'enable your servants to speak your word with great boldness' (v. 29) and then, 'stretch out your hand to heal and perform miraculous signs and wonders through the name of your holy servant Jesus' (v. 30). Focusing on God gave them a new perspective on what their priorities were. So Luke comments (v. 31) 'After they prayed, the place where they were meeting was shaken and they were all filled with the Holy Spirit'.[4]

This was not for a moment of spiritual ecstasy, or self-indulgence; but in order that they might proclaim God's word, proclaim the cross, to their generation. That is what Luke says in v. 31, 'they spoke the word of God boldly'. That was their priority. I trust it will be ours, as we focus on our Sovereign Lord.

Notes

1. For further discussion on the uniqueness of Christ, see chapter 10 of this book by Bishop Michael Nazir-Ali. See also Further Reading, below.
2. For Jesus' attitude to the Scriptures, and the classical evangelical view, see Further Reading, below. For the historic Church of England view of the supremacy and sufficiency of Scripture, see the 39 Articles of the Book of Common Prayer, especially Articles VI and XXXIV. For a discussion of the supremacy, sufficiency and inerrancy of Scripture, see John Stott's response to David Edwards in *Essentials: A Liberal-Evangelical Dialogue* (London, Hodder & Stoughton, 1988), pp. 83–106.
3. J. R. W. Stott *What is an Evangelical?* (London, Falcon Books, 1977), p. 6, based on his address at the conclusion of NEAC 2, Nottingham.
4. A letter from Canon Jack Wardle following this exposition raised the question: 'Whatever happened to Acts 4.31 and 32?' In response, I would say that I quoted it, although there was not time to explain it further. I agree with Wardle that 'signs and wonders' do sometimes

attest the bold preaching of the word of God – though in my view the transformation of people's lives is the most important demonstration of the power of God's word and Spirit. I also agree, therefore, with Wardle's words that 'the full gospel holds together Word and Spirit'. Somebody has said, 'if you listen to the word only – you dry up! If you listen to the Spirit only – you blow up! If you listen to the word and the Spirit together – you grow up!' There is truth in that.

John Stott's BST Commentary in *The Message of Acts* (IVP, 1990), to which I was particularly indebted in preparing this chapter, discusses some of these issues, and, in particular the so-called 'signs and wonders' teaching of John Wimber (see pp. 100–104). He asks three important questions of John Wimber's teaching on this subject:

1. Is it certain that signs and wonders are the main secret of Church growth in the Acts of the Apostles?
2. Is it certain that signs and wonders are meant by God to be 'everyday occurrences' and 'the normal Christian life'?
3. Is it certain that today's claimed 'signs and wonders' are parallel to those recorded in the New Testament?

Whatever our answers to these questions, we may well agree with John Stott's balanced summing up. He writes: 'If then, we take Scripture as our guide, we will avoid opposite extremes. We will neither describe miracles as "never happening" nor as "everyday occurrences", neither as "impossible" nor "normal". Instead we will be entirely open to the God who works through both nature and through miracle' (p. 104). We need to be equally balanced about a God who works through word and Spirit together.

Questions for Discussion:

1. What do we learn about prayer from Acts 4.23–31?
2. What do we learn about the beliefs and priorities of the early Church from Acts 4? In what way should these affect the beliefs, priorities and strategies of the local and national Church now?
3. What has the passage to teach us about our attitude to the so-called 'Toronto Blessing'?

Further Reading:

On the uniqueness of Jesus:
J. N. D. Anderson, *The Mystery of the Incarnation* (London, Hodder & Stoughton, 1978).
T. and P. Higton, *Jesus the Only Saviour; A Work Book on Christianity and Other Faiths* (Tunbridge Wells, Monarch, 1993).
J. Stott, *The Authentic Jesus* (London, Marshall Pickering, 1992).
C. Wright, *What's So Unique about Jesus?* (Eastbourne, MARC, 1990.)

On Jesus' attitude to the Scriptures:
D. A. Carson and J. D. Woodbridge, *Scripture and Truth* (IVP, 1983).
R. T. France, *Jesus and the Old Testament* (London, Tyndale Press, 1972).
J. I. Packer, *God Has Spoken* (London, Hodder & Stoughton, 1979; rev. edn, 1993).
J. W. Wenham, *Christ and the Bible* (London, Tyndale Press, 1972).

CHAPTER TWO

'Full of Grace and Truth'

Michael Baughen

'In everything may Jesus be pre-eminent.' This is our longing for our world, our country, our Church and our lives – may it also be so for our Conference together. It is an enormous encouragement and joy to look round at this great assembly of brothers and sisters in Christ, who share leadership in the Church, lay and ordained – readers, churchwardens, Parish Church Council (PCC) members, evangelists, youth leaders, home group leaders, parochial clergy, deans, archdeacons, bishops – all of us wanting to serve Christ more effectively.

We need each other, we need to strengthen one another, and hear one another. So, although there is much appreciation of the positive elements in the various evangelical emphases and groupings that exist among us, there is also considerable concern that we may lose our essential unity and pull apart at the very moment when it seems that God has given us so much opportunity for his gospel in our land.

The Islington Conference used to be the common

meeting-ground for us all.[1] The need for such a meeting has been shown by the overwhelming response to *this* Conference. Our ideas of a discussion-type conference had to yield to a speaker-packed conference because of the size.

However, we hope that the very fact of so many joined together in fellowship at the Conference will strengthen the oneness that we already have in Jesus Christ, and our unity as evangelicals in the Church of England, committed to making Christ known in this generation.

In this chapter, my burden is to call all of us who are evangelical leaders, lay and ordained, to be truly 'g' and 't' Christians, by which I mean 'grace and truth' Christians!

Grace and Truth

Truth without grace may be accurate and mind-changing but is so often repellent, hard, exclusive, arrogant and condemnatory of all who waver from it by even a hair's-breadth. Grace without truth, on the other hand, is initially magnetic, comfortable, soft and widely accepting but is then ineffectual, without saving or transforming power, and leading nowhere. But when we put grace and truth together we have the model of our Lord's ministry. *He* was full of grace and truth.

Truth *with* grace is attractive. It reaches the heart as well as the mind; it makes truth incarnate in the evidence of a life of attractive goodness. It stands by principle but handles it with love; it says, 'Sin no more' but makes the condemning stones fall to the ground; it draws people to Christ and attracts them into the fellowship of his Church. It has a firm centre and firm principles but soft edges; it has generosity of spirit; it welcomes the extravagance of the alabaster box and ignores the cries of 'waste'; it sits with the outcast and the socially unacceptable; it is far more positive than it is ever negative; it is far more concerned with saving than with condemning; it is far more ready to listen than to pontificate; it is far more concerned with what can be praised than in finding fault. Our Lord's wonderful ministry was like this; it has to be true of ours. We are to be 'g' and 't' Christians!

It was Moffatt who said: 'The religion of the Bible is a religion of grace or it is nothing – no grace, no Gospel'.[2] Grace cascades through the New Testament. Think of Ephesians. In chapter 1, Paul greets his hearers with grace; he speaks of the sonship conferred on us in Christ as 'by grace' and calls us to live to the praise of God's glorious grace. When he speaks of the wonder of our forgiveness through Christ's shed blood, he speaks of it as grace 'lavished upon us'. He is thrilled with the generosity of our gracious God. Then, in chapter 2, when he speaks further of the truth of the gospel, he gives us that marvellous phrase, 'By grace you are saved'.

Ephesians is really an overture of grace which affects every other issue, as it must do for *us.* As the letter develops there are a number of areas which emerge as part of the impact of grace. But before I go on to those, let me pause to reflect.

A Reflection

Some of us have been around for quite a number of years. Those of my generation are the products of Anglican evangelicalism in the 1940s to 1950s. We thank God for very faithful ministries which brought us to Christ, but Anglican evangelical churches were few and far between. The number of evangelical ordinands was between 7 and 10 per cent. There was a sense of being beleaguered within a Church that seemed to be dominated by non-evangelicals. It was inevitable that there was to some extent a hard edge and a distrust of all who did not share what we felt to be the only expression of the truth. Several things helped us to grow from that position. For many of us it was John Stott's starting of Eclectics which was the liberation.[3] Here the acceptance of the authority of Scripture was the one condition for joining. Then the discussion was wide open. There was no condemning of others.

It was in that trusting atmosphere that we were able to hear one another, respond to one another and look at some of the things which had become hard and fast rules within the evangelical Anglican world and yet did not really stand up to Scripture. We looked at very many issues and as our understanding of truth grew so we began to reach out into all sorts of developments. Theological writing developed, new ways of evangelism, a fresh emphasis upon expository preaching, new ideas of parochial strategy, pioneering in hymnody and music, in communication and in so many other ways, not least in care for the needs of the world and society. So the pace has continued through various Anglican evangelical conferences.

An Encouragement

Who could have believed back in the 1950s that there would be such growth? Who could have dared to believe *then* that in 1993 the evangelical theological colleges would contain 56 per cent of all male ordinands training in Church of England colleges? Who could have possibly foreseen the fact that we would actually have many evangelical archdeacons, deans and bishops and that there would be a strong evangelical representation within General Synod? Who could have foreseen the changing map where evangelicals would be seen working caringly and faithfully in a huge number of parishes of different traditions and bringing people alive to the word of God by grace and truth. Who could have foreseen the wonderful opportunities for evangelical gospel ministry in 1995? To those of us who have lived across the last 40 to 50 years it is the Lord's doing and it is marvellous in our eyes and so many of us here want to praise him from the bottom of our heart for what *he* has done.

There is a very real sense in which we may say together that the Lord has put the ball at our feet and if we falter now it will be a disaster and we shall stand ashamed before Our Lord. It is certainly not the time to pull out, but more than ever to *pull in.*

Some Marks of Grace and Truth in Ephesians

So let me return to Ephesians and to these emphases which do not just apply to us as evangelical Anglicans but ought to be evident amongst all who stand on Scripture. They are the means of blessing to the whole Church:

First, in the second part of chapter 2, Paul spells out that *the gospel is for the whole world:* The truth that God was saving the Gentiles as well as the Jews was revolutionary. It needed enormous grace to accept this world-vision of salvation. For us now it is basic in our thinking. We believe with all our heart that the gospel is for the whole world. We believe Christ Jesus died for all. We believe his atonement was the centre of God's self-giving love for the world. It is this that has driven the spread of mission across the world. Of course, it has not just been by evangelicals. Nevertheless, mission burns in the heart of the evangelical.

It is the belief that Jesus is the Saviour of the world and truly God of God, the Son of God, that makes us stiffen our stance in the growing debate over the uniqueness of Christ. The softness of apparent graciousness that now merely sees Christianity as one amongst many equivalent roads to God is seen by us as blasphemy of the Son of God. We are now going to have to stand up and contend for the uniqueness of Christ as we have never had to do before.[4]

Yet in all of this we must have the grace that goes with that truth, that can discern the good in others and other religious views and which values others as fellow human beings. They often have much to teach *us* and for *us* to learn, without compromising our stand.

And when we speak of the whole world we must mean the inner-city areas of our country or remote country parishes and areas to which evangelicals are often not so readily inclined to go. Just as the flame was carried out from Jerusalem by the early dispersion, so today the very fact that many evangelical clergy are in churches of different traditions is a form of dispersion which we should welcome and with grace should continue to take forward. Such evangelicals need enormous support from the structures and from fellow-evangelicals and are hurt by the near triumphalism of some big churches.

Let us resolve to see the *whole* world for Christ and the *whole* country for Christ, so that we do not allow the Church to draw back into a form of supermarket centralization in different towns with all the local outlets closed down. The need to overhaul our evangelism is so urgent.[5] Being a bishop of a diocese with 370 churches has given me a passion which has never left me for these 12 or so years in that service for my Lord. I long to see every church of every tradition alive in Christ. To this end I work, pray, preach, weep, care and give my heart for my Lord to whom I and all of us are accountable. Let us never lessen our passion for the *whole* land and for the *whole* Church of Our Lord.

Second, in chapter 3, Paul speaks of *true gospel service*. Paul saw himself as a recipient of God's grace for his evangelistic ministry. He did not appoint himself a leader. He saw his ministry of proclaiming the good news of the unfathomable riches of Christ as a sheer privilege. 'I am the least of all God's people', he said (v. 8). Isn't it a staggering thing that the living God has entrusted ministry to you and to me? I am not worthy to be a lay leader or a clergyman, let alone a bishop. Anyone who wants to find fault with this earthenware episcopal vessel can easily do so as they did with Paul and as anyone could do with lay or clergy leaders here. Our calling is overwhelming and people's expectations of us are often unrealistic.

It was Hooker who pointed out that 'we look for much more in our governors than a tolerable sufficiency can yield'.[6] The same can be said of a clergyman as well as of a bishop. We are all what we are in his service by grace alone. We have many weaknesses and failures and it is only by God's grace and by the daily impact on our lives of God's revealed truth in the Scriptures that most of us can go on. Arrogant ministers are a total denial of grace.

We know that the priority task of our ministries is evangelism. Even if we are not gifted evangelists as such, we are still to reach out with love and the Word. Hard evangelism shouts the truth in an ultimatum style; gracious evangelism shares the truth faithfully but in the spirit of love, of putting the arm round the hearer, with the gentleness of Christ. Gracious evangelism is adaptable in its methods, its setting and its language, but the gospel is *not* adaptable. Like Paul in Romans 1, we are not ashamed of the gospel because it *is* the power of God for salvation of everyone who believes.

It is because we seek to lead people to a decision, to turn to Christ, to accept the faith, and to respond to the Lord that we see results. It is this preaching for a verdict and leading people to a commitment which is a particular gift we can bring to the whole Church.

We also have a marvellous opportunity with those who come to us for weddings and baptisms and in the sadness of bereavement and suffering. Some ministers are impatient with their ignorance, but gracious ministers are able gently to lead them to Christ. Those of us who confirm see how many adults are coming to faith as a result of such careful and gracious ministry in all sections of our Church.

What is really thrilling in our day is that all over the country there are evangelicals engaged in imaginative evangelism, schemes of development and relevant strategizing for the gospel. In so many places it is being done with grace and is immensely attractive to people beyond evangelical circles and a help, therefore, to the whole Church. Sadly in those few cases where it is done in arrogance and exclusiveness it has the opposite effect. My brothers and sisters, let us never cease to burn with gospel fervour, but always with grace as well as truth.

Third, in chapter 4 vv.1–6, Paul stresses *the need for unity*: Paul had to *implore* the Ephesians to be truly one and to put up with one another's failings in the spirit of love. He called them, you remember, to spare no effort to make fast the bonds of peace in the unity which the spirit gives – the unity of one body. Paul's absolutely essential point is that this spiritual unity *exists*; it is where we start but not where we finish. The key issue of how we translate this into a doctrine of the Church is vital to us today. Our forefathers were far clearer about this than we are.[7]

In chapter 3 of his first letter to the Corinthians you will remember that Paul describes the separate parties within the Church as acting with the spirit of the world. He regards it as sin. Those who are 'of Apollos' or 'of Paul' are seen to be people of infancy in the faith and wordly in their attitude. It is not surprising that immature believers do that today. They will hold up the leader of their particular section as someone who can never be wrong. You could easily fill in the 'I am of' by all sorts of different movements, churches, emphases and clergymen with charisma. One hears it said, 'I am a such-and-such evangelical'. While the *positives* of the different movements or emphases are held on to, we can live together. It is when others are criticized and condemned that the different emphases become separate and even competitive camps.

Grace has to reach out, to learn and listen. Grace wants to see the best in the other rather than the worst. As Paul put it in 1 Corinthians 3, everything belongs to us and we all belong to Christ and Christ to God. In the light of Christ, all differences become very secondary and *he* becomes primary.

At this moment in our history as Anglican evangelicals we need to make every effort, as Paul commanded us. For instance, it would be wonderful if we all resolved that we would take the greatest care not to criticize a fellow Christian in public, in writing or in the press (by letter or article) without first ensuring that we truly understand and accurately represent their viewpoint and motives – preferably by talking and listening to them face to face. You will recall the problem John had with Diotrephes, mentioned in John's third Epistle. John describes Diotrephes as someone who enjoyed taking the lead, who laid nonsensical and spiteful charges against other leaders and who even expelled some Christians from his congregation. John says that he will tackle the matter *face to face.* It would be a wonderful clearing of the air in our unity for Christ if we resolved that instead of fanning innuendoes about others, repeating gossip or accepting mass-media reporting, we would first see whether we have the truth.

Our Lord prayed in John 17, 'May they be brought to *complete unity* to let the world *know* that you sent me'. In the light of that we need to drop our differences and have unity. There is a whole world out there without Christ; and a country mostly without Christ. As a television personality said to me recently, 'Everyone regards the Church as irrelevant and your internal disputes as *totally* irrelevant'. But we know that the gospel is never irrelevant and that is what the world needs to see and hear – *not* our differences.

May we, where it is needed, reforge unity in personal terms during our fellowship together. Can we apologise or forgive if that is necessary? Can we say, as John Wesley did to his rival George Whitefield, 'If your heart is as my heart, give me your hand'?

Fourth, from chapter 4 v.7, Paul stresses *the need for mutual upbuilding*. He emphasizes that each of us is the recipient of God's grace as part of the bounty of Christ. He urges us to recognize the different ministries and to see them all as there to equip God's people for His service and to build up the Body of Christ.

Here it is the truth that matters, so that we are not tossed by every wind of doctrine. Truth is immensely important; bases of faith are important; the Creed is important. Yet, although unity in the Spirit *exists*, unity in the truth is an *aim*. Verses 12–13 tell us that the Body of Christ is to be built up by various ministries '*until* we all reach unity in the faith and in the knowledge of the Son of God'. We have so much to go on learning and discovering.

We stand together under the supreme authority of Scripture. We believe in revelation. We believe in the preaching, teaching, expounding and sharing of the Word of God. We study it and meditate upon it. We need to hear each other in the interpretation and application of Scripture.

Together we are concerned to stand against and to reverse the full-scale liberal teaching which eliminates all revelation, has nothing to do with the fall, original sin, redemptive salvation, atonement, reality of the resurrection and even life after death. The most recent and pathetic attempt to describe the so-called Sea of Faith movement as still part of Christianity is the most offensive of all. It was G. G. Findlay who said years ago, 'We may hold divergent opinions upon many points of doctrine – and yet retain a large measure of cordial unity and find ourselves able to co-operate with each other for many Christian purposes. But when our differences concern the Person of Christ – it is at once felt to be fundamental.'[8] Exactly. This is the fundamental issue and is the most urgent one before us.

In the face of that challenge we need to minimize our very secondary differences and unite in the strength, relevance and power of the orthodox faith in the Trinity, the incarnation, the atonement, the resurrection, the second coming, eternal life and the lifegiving, transforming, empowering and gifting work of the Holy Spirit.

Thank God for all the individuals, groups and organizations that have developed our theological literature, scholarly writing and richly-varied publishing in recent years. We need to encourage our present-day theologians to come more and more into the open with us so that we can benefit more from them.

Let us also thank God for the many outstanding developments that bless the whole Church – of which the Church Pastoral Aid Society (CPAS), its youth organization and its media materials are a marvellous example, used with blessing in churches of almost all shades.

It is also so good that we have many more evangelicals now within the House of Bishops. What a difference from 1986 when we had the problems of the Nature of Belief Report.[9] It may be useful to reflect that only three out of the twenty-two bishops able to be present at this Conference were in the House of Bishops at that time. That was the *only* time that collegiality was ever *required.* Out of it has come a myth (which is amazingly believed by quite a lot of people) that the House works in some compelling or coerced collegiality. It was only that *once* and it rebounded in our faces. It would have been much better if there had been a minority report by the small number of three bishops who did *not* want to accept the full orthodox faith. Nevertheless, all that is nine years ago and what is important is the future and those who will, in God's mercy, be called into episcopal position and membership of the House of Bishops across the years to come. Who will be the bishops of the future? Certainly not, tragically, those who opt out of commitment to the Church of England in the next decade. Make it a constant matter of prayer.

Together, at every level of the Church, we must work for the upbuilding of the truth. Yet, even here grace must be present. Paul reminds us in verse 15 'to maintain the truth in a spirit of love'. Grace and truth, love and truth have to go together.

Fifth, from chapter 4 v. 17, Paul stresses *the need for holiness*: The other outcome of God's outpoured grace shown in Ephesians is in the arena of holiness. We are to model our lives in the truth as it is in Jesus. We are to be created in God's likeness, and Paul says that God's truth calls for an upright and devout life.

This often requires a face-to-face engagement. Instead of speaking falsehood about each other, which can be so easily done if at a distance or in the press, we are to '*speak* the truth to each other'. Similarly, anger has to be dealt with before the end of the day and that must mean meeting the other person. The thief is not to steal (the sin of theft is impersonal) but rather to give to those in need (which involves a personal action). We are not to be offensive in our talking but to bless those who hear us. We are not to grieve the Holy Spirit by refusing to be generous or forgiving or tender-hearted to each other. All these are marks of holiness which commend the Gospel.

Paul then turns, in chapter 5, to those marks which seem to dominate our present society as much as in his day – sex and money. Immorality, impurity, greed are 'improper for God's people', he says in verse 3. Instead, God's people should be marked out by lives of love, self-giving, thanksgiving, consideration for others, and (chapter 6) godly strength.

The report *Issues in Human Sexuality*[10] contains much that is excellent, such as the clear statement that 'there is in Scripture an evolving convergence on the ideal of lifelong, monogamous, heterosexual union as the setting intended by God for the proper development of men and women as sexual beings' (2.29); that 'God's perfect will for married people is chastity before marriage' (3.8) and that we need to help our young people to resist peer pressure to have the kind of sexual relationships which involve intercourse before marriage.

Since this Conference was planned and the brochure published, the issue of homosexuality has re-emerged yet again through the pressure of a very vocal lobby, representing (as recent reliable statistics indicate) a very tiny homosexual community in this country.

We have always distinguished homosexual orientation from homosexual practice. At Nottingham in 1977 we said, 'We believe homosexual intercourse to be contrary to God's law and not a true expression of human sexuality'.[11] In 1987 the General Synod motion was equally clear.[12] So is the biblical material in *Issues in Human Sexuality*.[13] That is the conviction that I defend and argue. It is, as far as I am aware, the conviction of almost all evangelical laity, clergy and bishops, and indeed the majority of laity, clergy and bishops in other traditions of the Church. Most of us who believe the decision to ordain women can be argued from the New Testament do *not* believe that validating homosexual practice can be argued from the New Testament but that it would mean a departure from Scripture and from the Church's historic moral tradition. Thus, a theological and ecclesial watershed would be reached in this matter.

There is widespread concern on this issue and it needs thorough discussion with prepared papers in a special conference – soon. It would give opportunity to *discuss* the Report *Issues in Human Sexuality*, including the question-raising pastoral section. Meanwhile I commend the excellent Cambridge Paper of June 1994: 'Homosexuality: finding the way of truth and love', and its request that 'the Christian community must respond to the issue of homosexuality and to homophile people in a way that combines love and truth, compassion and biblical integrity.[14]

However, we must not let this issue, which is about a

very small section of the community, deflect us from the many other issues of holiness and of practical action, as 'God's holy people' in spheres affecting large sections of the world's population, such as poverty, homelessness, hunger, refugees, abuse, conflict, the family and marriage. We also need more speaking and writing on such themes. I could suggest a good new book on Christian marriage![15]

Holiness is important in the lives of all Christians because it demonstrates the genuineness of truth and grace in our lives, and so commends Christ.

Conclusion

So, in conclusion, my sisters and brothers in Christ, let us lift our hearts and minds to the centrality of Christ and our oneness in his Body. We need him above all. To us to live is Christ. But we need each other; we need to hear each other; we need to drop the sniping denigrations and guerrilla warfare and concentrate on the positives which we can bring from our different groupings. We must long, as surely we all do, to see the whole Church of England grow and blossom for Our Lord.

Recently, a bishop, not of our tradition, wrote to me about this conference saying he was praying that it would set on fire the evangelization of our country. I thank God for that vision which surely we all share and which should inspire our meeting together.

Historians tell us that one of the reasons for the failure of the evangelical ascendancy in the early mid-1800s was that their success meant they pulled apart when they most needed to continue to pull together.[16] It is arguable that this has happened in every century since the Reformation. In the name of our one Lord, I beg you, don't let history repeat itself – for the fifth time!

As people of world mission, gospel service, unity in the Spirit, upbuilding in the truth and holiness of life, standing under the authority of Scripture and members of the Anglican Church, let us go forward *together* – I repeat, *together* – under the headship of Christ Jesus Our Lord and in it all let us truly be like *Him*, evangelical Anglican leaders who are truly 'g' and 't' Christians, full of grace and truth. In everything may Jesus be pre-eminent!

Notes

1. Normally an annual meeting in London. It last met on 5 March 1984.
2. J. Moffatt, *Grace in the New Testament* (1931, p. xv).
3. A private society for clergy under forty. For many years there were national conferences, and local groups met for fellowship and study.
4. Chapter 6 by Bishop Michael Nazir-Ali.
5. Chapter 7 by Bishop Gavin Reid.
6. Hooker, *Laws of Ecclesiastical Polity* Book VII, xxiv, 16.
7. Chapters 3 by Dr C. Baxter and 4 by Bishop Michael Turnbull.
8. G. G. Findlay, *The Epistle to the Ephesians* (London, Hodder), p. 250.
9. *The Nature of Christian Belief*, from the House of Bishops (London, Church House Publishing, 1986).
10. A statement by the House of Bishops (London, Church House Publishing, 1991).
11. The Nottingham Statement (CPAS 1977) R3, pp. 63f.
12. This Synod affirms that the biblical and traditional teaching on chastity and fidelity in personal relationships is a response to, and expression of, God's love for each one of us, and in particular affirms:

    (1) that sexual intercourse is an act of total commitment which belongs properly within a permanent married relationship,

    (2) that fornication and adultery are sins against this ideal, and are to be met by a call to repentance and the exercise of compassion,

    (3) that homosexual genital acts also fall short of this ideal, and are likewise to be met by a call to repentance and the exercise of compassion,

    (4) that all Christians are called to be exemplary in all spheres of morality, including sexual morality, and that holiness of life is particularly required of Christian leaders.

General Synod, November 1987 *Report of Proceedings*, Vol. 18 No. 3 pp. 955f. The full debate is in pp. 913–956.

13. See above note 10.
14. By Christopher Townsend, *Cambridge Papers*, Vol. 3 (1994), No. 2, p. 4.
15. Michael and Myrtle Baughen, *Your Marriage* (London, Hodder, 1994).
16. See the histories listed on page 10.

Questions for Discussion

1. Discuss the relationships of the two aspects of unity
    - in Ephesians 4 vv. 1–6, that we *are* one in Christ and have to work at it with love and forbearance
    - in Ephesians 4 vv. 12–13, that we are to help one another mutually to '*reach* unity in the faith'
2. What happens if we demand absolute agreement on all details of the faith before we have fellowship?
3. Discuss G. G. Findlay's statement: 'We may hold divergent opinions upon many points of doctrine – and yet retain a large measure of cordial unity and find ourselves able to co-operate with each other for many Christian purposes. But when our differences concern the Person of Christ – it is at once felt to be fundamental.'
4. What can we do to maintain our essential unity in Christ?

CHAPTER THREE

Leadership in the Church of England

Christina Baxter

There are some big questions to which we normally assume we know the answers, but which it is good to examine afresh from time to time, in the light of changing circumstances. I want to address one of them: Is it biblical to be Anglican, and specifically is it consistent with the New Testament to be a member of the Church of England today? Or, to put it another way, are the patterns of church life in the apostles' times and our own patterns identical, or contradictory, or in some middling position, recognizably similar?

Before I attempt to answer this question, I want to make it quite clear that if it turns out to be the case that it is biblical to be Anglican, I do not intend anyone to draw the conclusion that to belong to any other denomination is not biblical! That is a separate question altogether.

I want to answer that question by considering: What are the characteristics of New Testament church life?

The Gospel Proclamation

First it was founded on the proclamation of the gospel: whether that gospel was proclaimed *by* Jesus to be 'the kingdom of God is at hand; repent and believe the gospel' (Mark 1.15), or proclaimed *about* Jesus by his followers: that 'Jesus Christ is Lord' (Phil. 2.11), or summed up by Paul in more detail: 'For I delivered to you as of first importance what I also received, that Christ died for our sins according to the scriptures, that he was buried, that he was raised on the third day in accordance with the scriptures ...' (1 Cor. 15.3f) it remains the case that it is the gospel word of Jesus which precipitates confession of sin, and of Christ, and which creates the life of Christians together – the Church. Can Anglicans, can the Church of England, claim to be founded on the proclamation of the gospel? I believe we can. Let's look at a few ways in which we might show this to be the case.

At the Reformation, the Church of England did not claim to be a new church; it was simply the Christian Church which had existed from the very first proclamation of the gospel in this land, being reformed precisely in the light of the gospel which had become blurred and blunted through medieval Western accretions, but which was rediscovered by the reformers working with the original languages and, like Tyndale, dying to make possible our daily privilege of reading the Scriptures in the language with which we undertake our daily life. Our historical foundation is in the gospel, and that was in no way changed by the Elizabethan settlement or later adjustments.

The Anglican church has, as a key part of its inheritance, a pattern of common prayer, which continues in the modern liturgies to be predominantly biblical. We praise God in the gospel canticles of Magnificat, Nunc Dimittis etc.; we pray to God, calling on him in collects which begin again and again by reminding him of his acts or promises, e.g. 'O God, who by the leading of a star didst manifest thy only begotten Son to the Gentiles ...' (BCP collect for Epiphany). In our daily praying of morning and evening prayer, we read a lectionary which takes us through the greater part of the Scriptures, and in our public services we are accustomed to the regular preaching of the gospel. Our corporate spirituality is founded in the gospel.

The sixth article makes clear the Anglican attitude to the relationship between doctrine and Scripture:

> 'Holy Scripture containeth all things necessary to salvation; so that whatsoever is not read therein, nor may be proved thereby is not to be required of any man, that it should be believed as an article of the Faith, or thought to be requisite or necessary to salvation.'

Our church's belief is articulated through the historical creeds, Apostles, Nicene, Athanasian, not because they are historical but because they are considered to be valid expressions of the New Testament gospel faith: 'for they may be proved by most certain warrants of Holy Scripture' (Article 8). Our doctrine is grounded in the gospel.

By contrast, unless we are to claim that only one pattern of ministry is to be found in the New Testament and that that pattern is necessary to salvation (historically claims which were espoused by catholicism and by some presbyterian church polities, but not one that I can imagine any evangelical Anglican holding) we cannot lay on one another or on any other church the *requirement* to have a *particular* pattern of ministry.

Our ministers, deacons, priests and bishops are equally authorized to exercise ministry at their ordinations through the presentation of the gospel in New Testament or whole Bible volume. This massive change in the symbolism of the previous Western catholic rite, in which chalice and paten were presented to priests, remains a real division between Anglicans and Roman Catholics today.

In countless modern Church of England documents about topics as wide ranging as *Not Just for the Poor*[1] and *Senior Church Appointments*[2] (chosen at random from my overstocked shelves) we find attention to the biblical material relating to each area. And our instinct is biblical too; if there is a report which is weak in this area, it is soon pointed out by members of Synod; or its omission is noted with regret. Our continued reflection on how to be Christians with integrity in today's society is gospel orientated.

The Gospel Centre

Second, New Testament church life was centred on the saving crucifixion and resurrection of our Lord Jesus Christ. We see this in the typical sermons of Acts: 'this Jesus, delivered up ... crucified ... killed ... But God raised him up ...' (2.23f) and we hear Paul: 'For I decided to know nothing among you except Jesus Christ and him crucified' (1 Cor. 2.2). Taken together, these events were simultaneously the most perplexing and the most normative for Christian theology. For instance, it was very hard to understand how the crucified could in truth be the Messiah, and yet neither the facts of history nor the confession of faith proved susceptible to revision, so the New Testament becomes the record of how the early Church found a framework in the Old Testament in which both claims could be sensibly made. Cross and resurrection became normative because it was these events above all else which gave rise to the need for that way of talking about God which allows for differentiation within God's unity, and which eventually gave rise to trinitarian theology. Cross and resurrection require that because only a trinitarian theology can prevent us from saying: 'God in his totality is dead' or 'Jesus is only a human being after all' and the Church could not assent to either of those statements. The cross and resurrection were also normative for Christian living; the sign that a Christian was truly indwelt by the same Spirit who raised Jesus from the dead was that her life became patterned after the self-denying love of the cross (Galatians 5.16–26). Just how important the events of cross and resurrection are is reflected by the proportion of the gospel narratives which is given to them.

We know that, besides the verbal proclamation of these saving events, there was also the symbolic proclamations. When people came to faith, the death and resurrection of Jesus were seen in the waters of baptism:

> Do you not know that all of us who were baptized into Christ Jesus were baptized into his death? We were buried therefore with him by baptism into death, so that as Christ was raised from the dead by the glory of the Father, we too might walk in newness of life. (Romans 6.3ff)

Then they were continually manifested in the breaking of bread together: 'for as often as you eat this bread and drink this cup, you proclaim the Lord's death until he comes again' (1 Cor. 11.26). Cross and resurrection are at the heart of acts of worship which are characteristically Christian.

One obvious way in which we are centred on cross and resurrection is in our continued use of the same signs or sacraments. They are called gospel sacraments (Article 25) because they sign to us the gospel of the cross and resurrection of our Lord Jesus Christ. The preaching of this gospel is what creates the Church, not the Eucharist as is so often suggested in modern theology.[3] If either sacrament of the gospel is to be said to create the Church, we must say that that happens at baptism in which we are 'grafted into the Body of Christ's church' (Book of Common Prayer, Baptism of Infants). However, we certainly may say that the eucharist *renews* the Church since it reminds her that her whole existence depends on the one 'full, perfect, and sufficient sacrifice, oblation, and satisfaction for the sins of the whole world' by which she lives 'until his coming again' (Book of Common Prayer Communion Service, Prayer of Consecration).

Another obvious way in which we continue to be thus centred is in the keeping of the Christian year, in particular Lent and Holy Week. For forty days we walk with special consciousness in the self-denying way of the cross in order to prepare ourselves to celebrate Easter. For instance, we pray:

> Almighty God, whose most dear Son went not up to joy but first he suffered pain ... mercifully grant that we, walking in the way of the cross, may find it none other than the way of life and peace ... (ASB collect for Lent 3)

Moreover, in keeping Holy Week we retrace the steps of Jesus in the week which changed the world, and return to the very roots of our faith. Whether or not our local church keeps Holy Week, our prayer book and subsequent liturgical provision anticipates that we will be doing so and in this they are patterning the liturgy to correspond to the emphasis on the last week of the life, death and resurrection life of Jesus which we have already found in the New Testament.

The Gospel Context

A third characteristic of New Testament church life was that it understood the word of the gospel and the events of cross and resurrection in the light of the Jewish Scriptures, a way of thinking which it had learned from Jesus (Luke 24.45f), and which it did not abandon even when it had its own Scriptures to add to them. Indeed, it understood itself in relationship with the same God in Jesus as had made himself known through the covenants of old (Acts 7; Hebrews 1), and in some complex way New Testament Christians believed themselves to be in continued relationship with God's covenant people the Jews (Romans 9–11) even when they, the Jews, did not recognize the one whom the Church regarded as the Jewish Messiah (Acts 2.36) as well as the Saviour of the world (John 4.42).

This is crucially important, since justification by faith, the belief 'by which the Church stands or falls' is explained by Paul in terms of the unfailing covenant of God with Abraham, 'by whom all the families of the earth shall bless themselves' (Genesis 12.3). This covenant has been renewed in Jesus: in him God keeps his part of the covenant *and ours*, for God takes upon himself our humanity in Jesus, and obeys God perfectly. His perfect obedience becomes ours by faith. All our theology and thinking about the Church has to be done in the context of this old covenant made new by the blood of Jesus 'poured out for many' at Calvary (Mark 14.24).

All of the characteristics which I have already mentioned might be adduced to show that the Church of England continues this pattern; at the Reformation and at the Restoration settlement it was not only the gospels or even the New Testament which transformed our Church, but new light shed on the Old Testament and fresh ways of relating the testaments to one another which gave new theological perspectives. Our liturgy, lectionary, doctrine, ministry and current practice all adhere to this ideal.

The Gospel God

It was because the early Church found in Jesus, the same God, whom it already knew in the old covenant, that it came eventually to articulate a trinitarian faith which was required by the cross and resurrection, and was the logical outworking of its New Testament narrative frameworks and its prayers. For instance, Jesus, as he was baptized, received the Holy Spirit, and heard a voice from heaven 'thou art my beloved Son ...' (Mark 1.9–11). This highlights the need for differentiation within God. Equally, Paul prayed for his friends: 'The grace of the Lord Jesus Christ, and the love of God, and the fellowship of the Holy Spirit be with you all' (2 Cor. 13.14). This is found in less compact form in the overtly theological passages; read Romans 8 where Paul cannot explain the consequences of the gospel without reference to God, Christ, and the Spirit; or 1 Peter 1.2 to 'the exiles ... chosen and destined by God the Father and sanctified by the Spirit for obedience to Jesus Christ ...'.

The Anglican Church adheres to that same trinitarian framework, sometimes in more naive and less articulated forms than is even found in the New Testament (!), but its intention is to be trinitarian. It is my conviction that a group of people are rightly called 'church' when they are consciously trying to relate to the God and Father of our Lord Jesus Christ, through Jesus and by the power of the Holy Spirit, or the Spirit of Christ. The marks of the Church (one, holy, catholic and apostolic) can be just that, signs that it is present in better or worse form, but what determines whether it is church or not, is simply whether it intends to be trinitarian in its belief and life, that is, whether it is seeking to worship God in trinity and to allow its life to be shaped by the life of that God. By this measure the Church of England is rightly considered 'Church' however much it may need to be reformed, or alternatively, however Christlike it may be. Neither its evident sinfulness nor its evident holiness would 'deny' or 'prove' that it was Church. Since it is not the case in the New Testament, it cannot be the case for the Anglican Church that its works constitute its identity; only its relationship with God does. Thus the old debates about the identifying marks of the Church which have in the past separated us from other churches need no longer be barriers, but bases of discussion as to whether we are more or less faithfully being the Church which God calls us to be.

The Gospel Mission

Because of this understanding of God, mission was the essence of the New Testament Church. It was never considered simply to be the chief task of the Church, as though it could exist in some way other than apostolically. The New Testament Church knew that it was apostolic, or sent, or mission-orientated, because it was keenly aware that the Father had sent the Son (Gal. 4.4; John 13.3), himself the apostle (Heb. 3.1) and in like manner the Son sent apostles: 'as thou didst send me into the world, so I have sent them into the world' (John 17.18). Thus from the very earliest times, the disciples were sent on preaching and healing tours (Mark 6.7–12, 30ff; Luke 10.1ff), so it is no surprise that after the resurrection had reversed their gloom, they began again to preach in every place (see Acts). Indeed those who were filled with the Holy Spirit the sender (Mark 1.12), who is also the Spirit of Christ, should not be surprised to find themselves being made after the likeness of Christ, the one who was sent. Being apostolic, mission orientated is the logical consequence of being grounded in the trinitarian life of God himself.

Although there are high and low points in the Church of England's manifestation of this feature, I want to suggest some very significant contemporary emphases which argue that we continue in the apostles' tradition here. The first is the very fact that we call ourselves the Church of England, and organize our ministry in such a way that there is no-one who is outside of our parish structure. We recognize that we have a mission to every member of our society and we have so organized ourselves as to make that possible. That has been, and continues to be an act of self-giving love as between parishes, such as Paul calls for in Philippians 2. We do not often think of the parish share or the quota in this way, but I believe that it is no exaggeration to do so. It is the decision of each parish, and indeed each Anglican not to live to themselves alone but to take thought and practical action for the common good. That is not to maintain the ministry in every place as an act of defiance in an age of slim resources; rather it is a mission-orientated decision that there shall be no area where the gospel is not available to ordinary people. Moreover it is a truly loving act which, like the love of God, sets free as well as longing to live in increasingly sharing love with one another. It is loving; it loves the world so much that some parishes give far more than they keep, as well as other parishes giving more than they need to maintain their own ministry. It sets free, as God sets us free in Christ, so that we can choose how to respond to God and to one another.

Take a little parish which is a net benefitter from this arrangement. It is set free to make the gospel known in ways which are culturally appropriate to their circumstances, in the best way it can. It can ignore the proffered advice and help of other churches or Christian leaders, or it can accept them and benefit from them, maybe giving other kinds of riches which God has showered on them in return. This is a truly godly act, because it leaves the parish as much freedom as God has given to each individual; to act alone, or to accept God's and the Christian neighbour's help in mutual love, and accountability.

Thus even if my parish church may not be actively engaged with mission, I belong to a church whose structures mean that I cannot disengage myself from the mission to every other person which is the Church of England's vision. I do not want to disengage myself, but I do want to try to help all my Anglican friends to see that however complicated the system is, it is radically biblical, because it reflects the pattern of relationship we know that God has with us, and which Paul commends to each of us in Philippians. And I want to learn to be humble enough to know that I do not know best how to spend money to promote the gospel in other places, or even sometimes in my own place. We need to learn the same humility in this area as we have come to learn in relationship to the churches overseas. We have had to come to abandon our paternalistic attitudes, to learn to trust them to decide what is best for themselves because they alone know all the circumstances. Why cannot that same trust exist here between parishes and different levels of the church, I wonder? Is it because we have failed to pray for one another in our deaneries about our financial priorities and problems? ... because we have not thought about ways in which our human and other resources might be shared between churches? I would like to suggest that we think about six months of praying daily for any other Christian leader before we challenge them publicly – and it goes without saying that that only happens after private consultation (Matt. 18.15ff).

There is another manifestation of our missionary nature which is also very precious. It is our desire to be sent not only to individuals but also to our society as a whole. In this we have to remember that the New Testament Church understood itself as the inheritor of the Old Testament, because if we were to look only at the New Testament we might, wrongly, assume that the early Christians had no time for this. There are only hints at challenges to existing social patterns: John the Baptist to those who came to be baptized, and to Herod; Jesus' cleansing of the Temple; the persistent preaching of repentance by those called before magistrates in preference to their own self-defence; the insistence of the New Testament that we pray for society's leaders. They are few hints, but they were first generation Christians, and it is not until there are Christians in positions where the moral questions have to be posed and answered that we come to draw on the Old Testament pattern of calling political leaders to espouse the ways of God. I am thinking of the need to make clear today that there are Christian patterns of behaviour that our society would benefit from taking seriously even if society as a whole, or even a majority of our people, do not return to a living faith in Jesus Christ in our generation.

Let me give two examples: we have come to see more and more clearly the bankruptcy of trying to measure everything by cost-effectiveness in money terms, and the devastating consequences of a rampant individualism and meritocracy which suggests to those more fortunate that they have rightly earned what they have got (instead of teaching them, as in the older ways of thinking of the aristocracy, to see it as the gracious gift of a kindly providence, for which they will be called to account) and which leaves people who are inadequate to fend for themselves. I am not an expert in politics or social theory, but as a Christian I know that when God, the ultimate measure of all things, is replaced with something else, such as money, society is bound to go wrong.

Equally, when we think that we ourselves are the originators of our own good fortune, we have replaced our Creator God with the individual person. Brazenly claiming 'I did it my way' is also a recipe for disaster. Society may not choose to heed our warnings, but I believe that part of being sent into the world, being apostolic, is about applying the gospel to social trends as well as to individual souls. And that means having people at a national level who are the Church's prophets about these matters. A Board secretary working in Church House Westminster may not feel very 'prophetic', but she or he may be walking in the footsteps of Hosea, Amos, John the Baptist, William Wilberforce, or Florence Nightingale. So too may be a bishop marching with miners in protest at the destruction of their mines, their livelihood, the fabric of their family life, their own self-respect and dignity, all sacrificed on the altar of profitability.

There is another point to be made in connection with mission: we need to recognize that the Church of England has often been criticized for leaving mission to chance, or at least to the voluntary mission agencies which sprang up in relation to many different parts of the world. Whilst this may be a fair criticism, looking round the Anglican communion now, as I had the chance to do at the last Anglican Consultative Council, it is clear that, for a church that was not 'officially trying' it has been used under God to bring the gospel very powerfully to many different places. As we recognize this in previous generations it should give us hope that, as we have consciously committed ourselves to this task of evangelism in this decade, God can use us again in our generation and in our own land.

The Gospel Ministry

This brings me to another characteristic of the New Testament Church. Its ministry pattern was always flexible and pluriform, supremely it was always service ministry.[4] Moreover, authorized ministers always seemed to work in teams which were mutually accountable; the major distinction being between local and itinerant ministers. I believe that we can add: the criteria by which different patterns of ministry were assessed, was always a missionary one. Will this pattern of ministry help the Church to grow numerically, and in holiness? Was this not what the arrangements of Acts 6 were about? It is often referred to as the appointment of the first deacons, though deacons are not specifically mentioned there. Here was the Church characteristically wanting to set free those who had the ministry of the word, so that the gospel could go forward. And equally, what were the apostles doing when they appointed elders in every place, setting aside those who would be able to be guardians of Christ's flock, who could feed the Church, refuting the perversity of false teachers, and doing all this by the power of the Holy Spirit, and the word of God's grace?[5] Such principles relating to ministry may be transferable from one culture to another, and we may want to adopt them today in re-assessing our patterns of ministerial deployment.

We can no longer claim the simple consensus of the preface of the Ordinal: 'It is evident unto all men diligently reading holy Scripture and ancient Authors, that from the Apostles' time there have been these Orders of Ministers in Christ's Church; Bishops, Priests and Deacons'; for the wealth of New Testament scholarship suggests a more complex pattern, in which, for instance, it may not have been possible to differentiate between 'overseers' (bishops) and presbyters (later called priests).[6] Indeed the New Testament knows of other kinds of ministry, 'apostles, some prophets, some evangelists, some pastors and teachers' (Eph. 4.11), and I very much doubt if the first Christians could have guessed which would be the 'orders' which would survive from the New Testament period to today, or the later Christians conjecture which would be the 'orders' which would survive from the flowering of ministry forms immediately after the New Testament period.

We may want to ask some radical questions about whether our practice is as clear as our Ordinal. If we did a sociological study of Anglicanism in some places we would find that there are four orders: bishops, priests, deacons and catechists. Or, we might find that the Church of England has three orders in practice: bishops, priests and readers, since the diaconate is obviously disfunctional as presently practised. However we think about them theologically, we may well want to add evangelists into a pluriform ministry for today, and to do so in a way which makes clear that this is a central ministry for the Church's missionary purpose.

However, I think that we can be clear that the New Testament does contain oversight, eldership and service ministry so that the Anglican Church was right, through all the struggles of its formative period to determine to keep to the pattern of ministry which it had received. We would be naive to suppose that a bishop was the same in the first century as in the fifth, in the late middle ages, in the newly reformed Anglican Church under Henry, or reshaped under Elizabeth I. Indeed, any of us over thirty know that episcopacy has changed in our living memory. It is unlikely to be able to resist further change, any more than the order of priests has or can resist it.

We are, I believe, at a highly significant point in the Church of England's life, as far as patterns of ministry are concerned. What will it mean to be a biblical Anglican today in this regard? I think that it will mean at least this: that with the Reformers and classic Anglican leaders of previous centuries we will hold to the pattern of ministry, or order, which was there in the New Testament, and in the earliest subsequent churches: an order of presbyters, amongst whom some were made bishops, but who differed not in kind, but merely in jurisdiction from presbyters; and an order of deacons. We will keep this threefold order unless it proves impossible to reform it in such a way as to ensure that it serves the purpose which Christian ministry needs to serve, of helping the Church to grow, numerically and in holiness. Its reformation will be in the light of the Scriptures, as it was in the period of the Reformation, but we will be their true inheritors if we say, as they did, in effect, to some of their continental contemporaries, 'if it proves impossible to reform the threefold order, then the gospel imperative must take priority.'

This pragmatic decision was made in the context of discussions about the validity of the ministry of some of the Continental Reformers who had allowed ordinations of ministers without bishops. Where this was done because local Catholic bishops opposed the reformations which were demanded by the gospel, Anglican bishops accepted that these were exceptional times and that these ordinations were valid and acceptable in England without 're-ordination' actual or conditional. Norman Sykes cites the comments of Richard Field who suggested that 'wherein all bishops were extinguished by death or fallen into heresy' there should not be condemnation of 'those worthy ministers of God, that were ordained by presbyters in sundry churches of the world, at such times as bishops in those parts where they lived, opposed themselves against the truth of God and persecuted such as professed it'.[7]

But I doubt whether it will prove impossible to reform the Anglican ways in which episcopacy, presbyteral and diaconal ministry is exercised today!

For myself it is precisely that kind of issue which is at stake in the current debate as to whether 'extended communion' is preferable to reforming our ministry patterns. We are the inheritors of two very gospel-motivated systems: the first is the parish system of which I have already spoken. The second is the parish communion movement to which we can raise no objection since it insists that Christians live by the constant renewal which is theirs as they claim the benefits of Christ's passion. But our current financial and ordained ministerial resources do not allow every church to have a communion service every Sunday. Lay people have a deep desire for regular communion and are not accustomed to having 'communion by desire', that is, reminding themselves that God does not withhold Christ from those who sincerely desire to receive him. If, as Norman Sykes and others have shown, the Anglican pattern has always been to acknowledge that the gospel and the sacraments are essential, whereas the threefold order in ministry patterns is desirable but not essential for the life of the Church, then we have to consider whether we are well advised to change the nature of the service of Holy Communion in this way. It is suggested that it can be celebrated in one church so that the elements may be carried to other churches for people to communicate by receiving the elements without their service of worship including the customary words of institution. The question is whether it is better to change the communion service which was instituted by our Lord himself, or to change the ministry which has developed through different periods of the Church's history.

There are five clear possibilities:

1. ordain more priests, which may mean increase our giving levels to more realistic proportions, or increase the number of non-stipendiary ministers
2. teach people to expect communion less often
3. allow the whole church to say the words of institution at the communion service where no priest is present
4. license lay people, perhaps readers or churchwardens, to preside at Holy Communion, as they already do in some parts of the Anglican Communion
5. allow 'extended communion'.

As we continue to debate this we need to see that this is a gospel issue, because current proposals are suggesting that it is better to mask the cross which Jesus intended to make crystal clear in the broken bread and shared wine, rather than to reform our patterns of ministry in ways that are radical enough to guard the gospel nature of this sacrament.

But that is only one instance in a much broader debate. If we are true to New Testament criteria of ministry, we must be asking at every stage: 'will this pattern of ministry enable the church to grow – numerically and in holiness?'

The Gospel People

As we do that, we must adhere to another New Testament feature of church life. The New Testament church was radically egalitarian, believing that it could be that at the same time as it was ordered, and honouring to the God of order. It all flowed out of Calvary and through baptism into the weekly pattern of eucharistic life of the Church. Christ died for all: at the foot of the cross there is no rank, all have sinned and come short of the glory of God (Rom. 3.23). All alike are baptized into Christ's death (Rom. 6) and are graced with his new resurrection life, so there is here no distinction: 'neither Jew nor Greek, there is neither slave nor free, there is neither male nor female, for you are all one in Christ Jesus' (Gal. 3.28). That is why it is an offence against the Body of Christ to eat the Lord's supper as if there could be distinctions between rich or poor (1 Cor. 11.17ff). St Peter learned early that 'God is no respector of persons' (Acts 10), and so the Holy Spirit could be given to God-fearing Gentiles before they had even been baptized. Equally, the sovereign God freely disperses his gifts of 'apostles, prophets, evangelists, pastors, teachers' (Eph. 4.11) for the corporate good.

Thus we are forced to take seriously – much more seriously than some of the Church of England's statements occasionally do – the dispersal of the Holy Spirit throughout the whole Church of God, so that the development of ministerial order must never be done in such a way as to demean or to ignore the ministry of the whole people of God. Is the deacon a person of prayer? So too are the whole people of God. Does the bishop have a responsibility to make the gospel known? So too does the whole people of God. Does the presbyter/priest take Christ with her or him into the sick visit or the counselling situation? So too does any member of the people of God, for the Spirit of Christ dwells within the lay person as well as within the ordained minister.

But this is not an entirely new concept for the Anglican Church. Since its inception it has always, though in ways that are very different now from its beginnings, allowed for the proper participation of lay people, bishops, priests, and deacons in the Church's affairs. This is currently expressed through parochial church councils, deanery and diocesan synods, as well as at General Synod level. Whether we have a right balance between the different parts of the Body of Christ is something which we need continually to consider, but the fact that everyone can potentially contribute something to the life and decision-making processes of our Church seems to me to be in line with the New Testament emphasis of all participating according to their gifts. As we do this we need to keep in mind the very real danger, highlighted by the report *All Are Called* of thinking that the normal Christian ministry is church-focused rather than world-focused.[8] Decreasing numbers of stipendiary clergy can mean that lay people get sucked into more and more churchy tasks, by centripetal forces which are clean contrary to the gospel which would have us be centrifugal.

The New Testament can work quite happily with the double notion of differentiation and unity, and although we may not be so adept at this, there nevertheless is something in the soul of Anglicanism which recognizes that schism is a very serious thing, and that wherever possible we should find ways of staying together even when we differ. Gifts, tasks, spheres of work, conscience etc. may cause differentiation between Christians in the New Testament, but that never breaks the unity which exists between them because they have been baptized into Christ. They *are* one body. Indeed, some differentiation is *so* that unity may be promoted. This is the message of Ephesians 4: different gifts are

> for the equipment of the saints, for the work of ministry, for building up the body of Christ, until we all attain to the unity of faith and of the knowledge of the Son of God ... speaking the truth in love, we are to grow up in every way into him who is the head, into Christ, from whom the whole body, joined and knit

> together at every joint with which it is supplied, when each part is working properly, makes bodily growth and upbuilds itself in love. (4.12–16)

The image is that at every point where our different lives touch one another, there are to be wholesome joints which work well and enable the body to function properly, so that a joint is not a painful place of mutual pressure, but one where each bone supports the other in healthy distinctiveness. Such differentiated unity is most clearly seen in God the Holy Trinity, whose unity is by no means spoilt by the differentiation of Father, Son and Holy Spirit.

If there can legitimately be differentiation of function in ministry, it must be so that the unity of the Church is better fulfilled, than if the Body of Christ were all ear, or nose. There is here a contradiction, a paradox, or a dialectic in our thinking (and in that of Paul before us) which can only work if, like a cat's cradle, we can keep the tension between: 'on the one hand' and 'on the other hand'. For it is true that we are all equally children of God, saved by Christ and inspired by the Holy Spirit. But it is also true that we are not equally mature children, equally living out of the truth of our new identity in Christ or identically gifted by the Holy Spirit. So when we come to choose our leaders, we naturally choose mature children of God, who have passed from milk to solid food (Heb. 5.11–14), and who have gifts appropriate to the tasks to which they are called.

Perhaps for these reasons, we can be forgiven for slackening the tension, and for being overawed, as I sometimes am, when I look at some of our bishops and sense their holiness; their deep spirituality, their evident life of prayer; or when we benefit from some of their teaching ministry, or recognize what immense changes for good can come about in a diocese as a result of a faithful ministry, and then we may want to say, in that famous phrase, that 'some are more equal than others'. But that is not true, for their holiness is to spur us on to similar holiness; their spirituality is to enable us to grow in grace, and their teaching ministry is to enable us to be more effective in the toolshop, in the playschool, on the dole, at our studies or in our retirement. God has given them those gifts *for our sake,* though as he is extraordinarily economical the gifts are also for them to enjoy.

If we are going to continue to expect differences between the ministries of the whole people of God; within the priesthood of all believers, then we need both to explore new ways of developing distinctive diaconal ministry which facilitates the ministry of the laity rather than diminishing it; and of giving and receiving authority within the Church. All those who are ordained to the threefold order have been given responsibility, which remains at the same time the responsibility of God, and of the whole Church. If they are to exercise the leadership which we ask of them, then they must be given by God the charismatic authority of person which enables them to exercise this effectively; and they must be given by the Church the authority to get on and do the job, always within the framework of mutual support and accountability. We have come a long way since a bishop in the Church of England arranging for the clergy to hold a synod felt he had to make it clear that there was only one vote in the synod, and that was his own. 'The general mind of the clergy ... is usually sound and wise; but when all this has been said the bishop has the first and last word.'[9] But we must also recognize that the authority of Jesus himself was always offered freely and never forced on people; only over the demons did he exercise absolute authority; his was always a gracious authority, however firm and clear in discipline.

I asked at the beginning whether it is biblical to be Anglican, or consistent with the New Testament to be a member of the Church of England. I hope that I have shown that it is. We are more accustomed to hearing of places in our church life where we fall short of some biblical or other ideal, and we are all aware of those. Nothing in what I have said is meant to suggest that I am blind to those places, or want to fall away from the *semper reformanda*, 'always being reformed' principle which is so important in the in-between times while we wait for the return of the Lord Jesus Christ.

There are several reasons why this is so important. One is human frailty which means that however good our attempts at living the Christian life, we can remain blind to the calls which the gospel makes on us. This needs to be put right as we are reformed by the Spirit of God in the light of further reflection on Scriptures. An outstanding example of this would be the Church's decision to abandon slavery, but there are countless other little reformations happening in the ordering of our parish church life all the time. Recent examples might be the genuine repentance which was expressed in General Synod when we had read and then debated the report of the Board of Social Responsibility on 'Ageing'.[10] Our structure may not yet reflect our determination not to be 'age-ist', but our behaviour individually has begun to change.

There is another reason why it is so important to be open to constant reform, and that is that the world changes, and our generation lives in times that are changing perhaps more swiftly than ever before because of information technology. The gospel has to be expressed in ways that are culturally appropriate. The New Testament Church learned that lesson very early when it struggled with the questions about the terms on which Gentile Christians could be admitted to the fellowship, and took the radical decision that their terms might be different from those of Jews (Acts 15). We have to be constantly reforming the Church so that it communicates the gospel in all the cultures and sub-cultures in which Christians live. Much variety between Christian communities may be a mark of their integrity rather than a mark of failure, as is sometimes alleged.

We will also want to change and be reformed as we continue to grow in understanding of the gospel, especially as we learn it afresh from Christians of other traditions, times and places. For instance, a South African priest summarized what the Church of the Province had learned through the hard times of apartheid as 'reconciliation is not part of the gospel; it *is* the gospel'. Our preaching will never be effective if we do not live our message. We in the Church of England know that God has given us 'the ministry of reconciliation', Paul tells us in 2 Corinthians 5.18. Intellectually it is very clear, but part of our reformation will be when we begin to allow this to be part of our daily living.

Finally there is outright sin which means that our originally good systems need to be reformed when they become corrupted by our selfishness. Despite our need for constant reformation, because Christ is at work among us, we may rightly expect to see some signs of his presence as well as signs of our continuing need of grace. My hope is that we will be able to recognize what God is doing among us and thank him for it at least as often as we bewail either our own sins, or those of others. It is, after all, his Church, his Body which we criticize, and for which we bless God.

Notes

1. *Not Just for the Poor,* BSR report on the welfare state, GS 756, 1986.
2. *Senior Church Appointments,* Working Party report GS 1019, 1992.
3. Contra Henri de Lubac and John Zizioulas. See Paul McPartlan, *The Eucharist Makes the Church* (Edinburgh, T & T Clark, 1993) for a recent exposition.
4. Cf. Hans Küng, *Why Priests?* (1972)
5. So St Paul to the Ephesian elders. See Acts 20.28 to end.

6. See for instance the Roman Catholic scholar Raymond Brown: 'Let us follow the common scholarly opinion, that, where they existed in the post-Pauline churches, presbyters and bishops were for all practical purposes the same, that as a group they were responsible for the pastoral care of those churches.' *Priest and Bishop: Biblical Reflections* (London, Geoffrey Chapman, 1971), p. 35.
7. R. Field, *Of the Church* Bk III, pp. 154–71, cited in *Old Priest, New Presbyter* (Cambridge, Cambridge University Press, 1956); cf Paul Avis, *The Church in the Theology of the Reformers* (London, Marshall Morgan and Scott, 1981).
8. General Synod Board of Education, *All Are Called* (London, CIO, 1985).
9. Cyril Garbett, *The Claim of the Church of England* (London, 1947), p. 108.
10. Board of Social Responsibility, *Ageing* (London, Church House Publishing, 1990).

Questions for Discussion

1. Where do you think the Anglican Church (or the Church of England) is most consistent with biblical patterns of church life?
2. Where do you think that the Anglican Church (or the Church of England) is most in need of reformation?
3. Can you think of ways in which our ministry patterns could be more apostolic, that is, more mission-oriented?

Further Reading

Paul D. L. Avis, *The Church in the Theology of the Reformers* (London, Marshall Morgan and Scott, 1981).

Tim Bradshaw, *The Olive Branch* (Carlisle, Paternoster Press, 1992).

Colin Kruse, *New Testament Foundations for Ministry* (London, Marshall Morgan and Scott, 1983).

CHAPTER FOUR

Issues of Ecclesiology

Michael Turnbull

Introduction

The letter to the Ephesians begins with the great themes of the sovereign power of Christ, the miracle of his free gift of grace and the response of holy living. By chapter 3, the writer is preparing the way for the practical outworking of these great themes. He speaks of bringing the purposes of Christ to light and putting them into effect. He speaks of the essential worship of the Church, of the humble service that is due to and through each member of the Church and of the imperative of taking the good news of the gospel to the whole world, both Jew and Gentile.

As Chairman of the Archbishops' Commission on the Organisation of the Church of England I have, of course, been reflecting on the relationships between the various bodies of the Church. We have had some excellent discussions in the Commission and we find in the institutions of the Church much to cherish and much to thank God for. There is also much we need to think about further. We are still in the process of working out our recommendations. I therefore ask you, please, not to try to discern the mind of the Commission from what I say here.[1] Today, I want simply to share with you my own reflections about what I see as the institutional nature of the Church of England as the context in which we carry out the work of worship, service and evangelism.

At the beginning of each meeting of the Archbishops' Commission on the Organisation of the Church we begin with this prayer which reflects those themes from Ephesians.

O God,
in whose sovereign power
rests everything in heaven and earth.
Take hold of your church today,
that in the organization of its work,
the use of its resources
and the planning of its strategy,
it may serve this nation with humility,
witness to your love with boldness,
and worship you in holiness.

Through Jesus Christ our Lord. Amen.

We thus acknowledge the sovereignty of God and we claim that grace which can take hold of today's Church if we use wisely the resources that he has abundantly given us.

The Present Opportunity

There is no doubt in my mind that God has given us a window of opportunity at this stage in the life of the Church of England to shape it for its essential tasks. Those include worldwide obligations through its partnership in the Anglican Communion – its share in the mission of the universal Church. It also embraces an indispensable role carried out through national and diocesan structures.

Nevertheless, I believe the mission of the Church is most clearly and gloriously seen in the parishes. They do not represent the whole of the Church's work, but it is true to say that without them the main purpose of the Church would be lost. The structures of the Church must, therefore, be, and be seen to be, the servants of the local congregations and the parishes which are the setting of their ministry. If the structures fail in that role, the Church is impeded in its mission. The work of the Commission is therefore to propose means whereby the Church can fulfil its task at the cutting edge of its ministry in the parishes.

The Threefold Task of the Church

The Epistle to the Ephesians, reflected in the prayer for the Commission, points to the threefold task of the Church of worship, service and witness.

Worship

Christian worship reacts to a God who has revealed himself – in creation, in history, and supremely in the person of Jesus Christ. The traditions of the Church of England have centred on liturgical forms which have given prominence to Scripture, as an authoritative channel of God's revelation in Christ, and to tradition, as the inheritance from the Church down the ages. These have been embodied in the Prayer Book, the result of the Elizabethan Settlement, and in the twentieth-century liturgical revisions of the Alternative Service Book. They remain indispensable to the identity of the Church of England.

It is part of the legal responsibility of the Church of England to provide a place of worship in every parish. All who reside within the parish have rights of entry. Equally, every parish is required to provide regular worship in its place of worship and this must include provision for the regular celebration of the sacrament. Thus, it is an obligation for every parish to have the services of a minister who will not only conduct Sunday worship, but also be available for the essential work of teaching which will lead people to baptism in faith, and to the marking of every stage of Christian growth and human experience, with a recognition of God's Lordship.

The provision of worship in every parish is a requirement which the Church gladly accepts, but it has an important effect on the organization of the Church and in the use of its resources. It underlies the fact that the Church of England cannot be organized on purely economic grounds, but on considerations based on service to the community as a whole and its obligations under God and to the state. The Church of England, for instance, cannot pull out of parishes which do not 'pay' and simply concentrate on 'successful' areas. The presence of the Church, indicated by a place of worship and ministerial leadership, should be based on local need rather than the accidents of history. Population changes since the Victorian era may require adjustments in the level of provision in some areas. Resources may need to be moved away from places that have experienced depopulation, whether in urban or rural settings. More provision may need to be made in new towns and housing estates which have grown in the last 50 years. But the criteria for such changes should not be the strength of the Church, either in congregational size or financial viability, but the need of the area – spiritual, economic and social. The provision of Church of England liturgy, ministry and building in every parish remains an accepted part of its mission from which it would not wish to abdicate.

Service

Service to the community is the second obligation of the Church of England's tripartite mission. The Church of England's response to this is the ideal of a servant people in every community, with a leader who presides at that worship and leads them out in service. The service which is offered is indiscriminate. Christians are required not only to care for each other, but for anyone in need, regardless of status, creed or race. Clearly, such a programme cannot be cost-effective nor can its results be adequately appraised.

But we live in an England today that does not easily link locality with community. One response to these changes is to suggest the dismantling of the parochial system. Indeed, some activity suggests that this is happening. Particularly in suburban areas, some parishes have attracted large congregations from a wide area, and it is probable that significant numbers of worshippers in many parish churches no longer live within the parish boundaries. That is a process which is likely to continue and no law or structural change is likely to alter it even if that were desirable.

Nevertheless, I believe that the parochial system has sufficient theological and social merit for it to continue as fundamental to the Church of England's strategy for service. The gospel of redeeming love and sacrifice must take root in the immediate neighbourhood. A local church would not be true to its calling if it sent money and people across the world, and neglected the needs of the people down the street. A Christian congregation should at least be attempting to create a community of mutual love and care, even where social forces have made it impersonal. That is not to say that the parochial system cannot be subject to sensitive modification.

We should not romanticize and have expectations of the parochial system which are more consonant with an England of the eighteenth century. In order to function in the twenty-first century, the parish and the minister have to recognize that serving can only be adequately attempted in partnership with others. It requires the recognition that other churches and institutions are sometimes better placed to take the lead. It demands patience in developing local mechanisms where partnerships can be forged. In other words, it means abandoning the worst features of parochialism while valuing the personal and the local.

This also has implications for the kind of ministers that we need. Each minister has to recognize that there are now many people in the parish who are better equipped than he or she is to offer some kinds of service. Others are capable of being trained to offer practical, pastoral and spiritual help as part of the mission of the whole people of God. This means that some of the traditional roles of the clergy are disappearing and the local minister needs to be trained to train, to set up networks, to build up teams of ministries and to be the servant of the servants. Thankfully, much of this is already in place and operating well but it demands a special kind of resourcing if service is to be developed as a main strand of the Church's mission strategy.

Witness

The third element of the Church's mission is witness. The disciples were to witness to Jesus and to his resurrection (Acts 1.8 and 22). The first apostles derived their authority from being present at an appearance of the risen Lord and they were to exercise that authority by teaching what they had experienced and by making new disciples. They witnessed the Lord and they witnessed to the Lord.

One of the more potent ways by which the early Christian witnessed was by a distinctive lifestyle, both individually and corporately. They frequently failed in both settings, hence the concentration of teaching in the epistles about appropriate Christian behaviour. But they succeeded sufficiently (for example Acts 2.42–47, where worship, service and witness are very apparent) to attract others to the Faith.

Witness, therefore, implied holiness of living, including forgiveness and restitution, teaching the Faith, and evangelism, the latter being the outcome of the first two. It is important to note for our purposes that, from the first century, problems arose about the resourcing of local congregations – financially and in terms of authority and teaching. Federations of congregations grew up centred around the travelling apostles. Though they developed their own styles against different social backgrounds, they were both supported and disciplined to ensure that there was some consistency of teaching. A congregation that is isolated from authority and the support of others is threatened by idiosyncrasy and division.

In this discussion about the basic tasks of the Church – worship, service and witness – five fundamental principles emerge:

- The tasks are clear but allow for a wide variety of application depending on particular opportunities and constraints.
- The tasks are best carried out at local level but must also be viewed in a wider context if they are to be carried out effectively.
- The local Church must seek to be efficient, in terms of considered action and the making of choices on the basis of sound thinking. But it must not necessarily be cost-effective. By its nature, the gospel of love is sometimes extravagant.
- Wherever possible the local church must have freedom to make its own plans for carrying out the basic tasks, but it requires authority outside itself in order to retain opportunities for fellowship with the wider Christian community, in which it finds its identity.
- The local church must be responsible for its own resources but also be prepared both to give and receive from the rest of the church as circumstances demand.

It is to the question of these resources that I must now turn.

The Resources of the Church

Grace

The chief resource of the Church is the grace of God. No amount of structure and organization can put the Church right if, at every level, it is not turning to God for his provision. He is the Creator and sustainer of the Church. It looks to God for planning, strategy, resource and purpose. The means of God's grace come from Jesus Christ himself, the founder of the Church. The channels of his grace are Scripture and sacrament as received and shared within the fellowship of the Church.

The whole people of God look to him in these ways for their resourcing. At the heart of church life there is a continuing process of becoming aware of God and his purposes; of growth and change which makes the Church more like the body God wants it to be; of risk and exploration into the unknown. The basic resources which God offers are dynamic and presuppose a Church that is in pilgrimage and process. Each generation and each setting has to be ready for the surprises of God and to be open and flexible enough to respond to them creatively and thankfully.

That is why the present time in the life of the Church is such an opportunity. Now is a time when we can review our resources and adjust the mechanisms by which we assemble and distribute them – in a clear and explainable way yet leaving sufficient flexibility for responses to new invitations which God issues and for which he will continue to provide resources. Within that context of grace the Church has three main sets of resources – people, buildings and money. They are interdependent and as a whole they are essential for the Church to carry out its tasks.

Human Resources

The people resource is the whole body of Christians who

belong to the Church. Through the sacramental act of baptism, in which God's saving action has its outward and visible form, and through the inward conversion of heart and will, people are not only made members of the Church, with access to its teaching, sacraments and fellowship, but are also commissioned to witness to their faith by their lives. They are told to 'fight valiantly under the banner of Christ' and to 'shine as a light in the world'. How effectively they are able to do this will depend on the faith and confidence they gain within the life of the Church, and the opportunities they take for service and witness in the world in which they live. Hence it is vital that resources are directed to teaching, guiding and supporting.

Ephesians 4 describes the recognition of this resource as gifts to the Church. Whether they be in administration, finance, leadership, care, teaching or evangelism, they represent the workforce of the Church and need training, authorization and deployment, though this is a complex task since levels of commitment and individual abilities vary.

Out of the whole body of believers, the Church chooses ministers with particular authority and defined tasks. While the local congregation will be the essential source of such ministry, and vocations will continue to arise out of the prayer and deciphering of the local congregation, because people move around so much and because strong Churches may often wish to help the weak, there needs to be accepted and understood mechanisms whereby ministers are selected, trained and deployed. In some cases this will involve also pay and housing. Ideally, these mechanisms will involve both the local church and the wider Church in order that their ministry is acceptable and also has some kind of consistency.

The received tradition of the Church of England is that responsibility for seeking out, training and authorizing these ministries rests with the bishop. In his region or diocese he is the focus of unity of all the local congregations.

It is his duty to provide them with the resources they need and to ensure that their worship and teaching have a continuing identity within the universal Church.

In the devising of structures to assemble and distribute resources it is clear, therefore, that the bishop must be a key figure. He must exercise his role in consultation with the local congregations in his diocese, with his fellow bishops and the lay and ordained people of the national Church. Such consultation can only be successful when all concerned are clear about objectives, have accurate information about resources, and are in agreement about what decisions are made where. But in the context of this consultation, bishops have a right to expect a respect and loyalty which is neither blind subservience nor arrogant contention. Biblical leadership functions best when there is a high doctrine of obedience and loyalty.

Financial Resources

This consultation, communication and decision-making is carried out by the synodical structures and it succeeds more than we sometimes give it credit for. Because of the cumbersome nature of the structures of the Church, it has not been possible, or no-one has seen it as their responsibility, to construct an overall financial strategy which takes into account the purposes of the Church, its current and future obligations to its paid and pensionable servants and its ambitions and aspirations for carrying out its mission.

It is part of the task of the Archbishops' Commission to make proposals which would ensure that a financial policy can be agreed and executed in such a way that the needs of the Church can be given an order of priority, and a clear indication of them given to those who contribute to, and manage the Church's money at all levels.

I say at all levels because the history and particular vocation of the Church of England provides special opportunities for service outside the local congregation and at regional and national levels. For instance, a significant proportion of the local minister's time is spent in pastoral work outside the immediate membership of his congregation. He, or she, visits hospitals, buries the dead, prepares for marriages, and is available for counselling and care.

Important parts of the Church's mission can only be carried out at national level. Worship, service and witness may still summarize this aspect of the Church's work. If the national responsibilities of the Church are working well, it forms a powerful and influential stage setting on which the parishes can carry out their mission. So the national Church needs its own resources. The structures of the Church being the means by which the resources are assembled and distributed face in two directions. As well as seeking to enable the local church fulfil its mission, the structures must also support the national church.

It is, perhaps, at this point that loyalty to the history and ethos of the traditions of the Church of England is most severely tested. When the Church could rely on a high percentage of its income arising out of historic resources, decisions about the deployment of those resources could be made at national and diocesan levels. But that percentage has drastically fallen in recent years and more and more of the Church's total income is derived from 'live' giving at the parochial level. There has been a consequent shift of power to the local church. In itself that is good for the long term well-being of a contemporary church. In other words those who are praying together day by day and whose worship and witness is grounded in the reality of the local, are now asked to provide the finance whereby the whole of the national church can carry out its mission.

There is, however, an inherent danger in this shift and it is making itself apparent in the attitudes of a significant number of parish congregations. Those attitudes are formed by a particular understanding of the Church – hence the emphasis in these pages of rediscovering an acceptable and workable ecclesiology for the Church of

England. A local congregation cannot be truly Anglican if it fails to recognize the financial needs of the world-wide Church, including that of other parishes within the diocese and national church. That will include parishes of other traditions within the Church of England.

The question therefore arises, can a parish pick and choose whether it supports the whole Church through the normal channels of the Church of England? Clearly, if a large number of parishes followed their own preferences, the result would be chaos and the allocation of resources within a national and diocesan strategy would be impossible. In other words, it would result in nothing less than the collapse of the Church of England as we know it.

I have some sympathy with a committed and hard-working congregation which believes it is subsidizing apathy and lack of vision in another. But is financial blackmail the right way of making this protest? It may be more tiresome but surely the scriptural way, and the way more true to the traditional concept of the Church of England, is to challenge the wider Church in the context of love and fellowship and using the synodical mechanisms at its disposal.

Buildings Resources

While church halls, offices and vicarages remain an important part of the Church of England's buildings economy, it is our parish churches which constitute its more vital element. It is there that the local church meets for worship, is inspired for service and is educated for witness. In many localities the church building is a powerful signal of the Church's presence. Many who use the building only for rites of passage have, nevertheless, an affection for the parish church. Many will give to keep the church roof on but not to pay the vicar.

In addition, many non-local heritage and conservation lobbies may have an interest and press hard for as little change as possible to buildings which provide real problems for modern liturgical use. The lobbies may be perfectly laudable and be supported by legislation.

But with all these pressures, what hope is there of developing a strategy for buildings as resources for the threefold task of the Church? Certainly the Church cannot operate like a high street bank and simply close and sell off church buildings which are no longer needed in a purely utilitarian sense. There is, however, scope for taking an overview of church buildings which would consider the obligations to the parochial system, our responsibility to heritage matters *and* our needs as a church in a missionary situation. At present there is no clear mechanism for doing this. If such a system was available, at least we should be able to devise a long-term plan and engage in a variety of partnerships which could put it into effect.

Conclusion

You will understand that I have been seeking to explain briefly how important it is that the overall policies of the Church of England can be clearly stated and effectively communicated. At the moment, there is widespread confusion. Some will see the Archbishop of Canterbury as being the person who should be able to speak for the Church of England. Some look to the Church Commissioners as being the powerful financial voice of the Church though, in fact, they are accountable to Parliament. Others would regard General Synod or the bishop in synod in his local diocese as framing policy and making decisions about resource allocation. For others the all-important decisions are made at local level, though, even there, the Parochial Church Council and the leadership of the local congregation would expect to exert some influence, for instance, on a network of house groups rather than let all decisions be made there! It is this muddle which is the target of the Archbishops' Commission.

We see our task to make proposals for structures and mechanisms within the Church which will

- Support, supply and affirm the local church in its mission.
- Ensure a continuing identity for the national Church, particularly in its teaching, worship and order.
- Manage efficiently the financial and legal framework in which the Church has to work.
- Witness, clearly and sensitively, to the nation.
- Communicate the purposes of the Church internally and externally.
- Sustain a church under change.

We do not underestimate the complexities of this task. Indeed, the more evidence we collect, the more complex it becomes. However, the Commission has reached a point where it is beginning to shape outline proposals. We will not answer every question, certainly we will not please everybody. In the end, the Church of England, like the early Church, has to hold in tension the authority of individuals and the truth as it is revealed within the whole Body of Christ. But, as I have said, I believe that the Archbishops have chosen an opportune time, when the Church as a whole sees the need for change and has the will to think and plan in a radical way. Without that determination nothing that the Commission proposes will be implemented. Already in the Commission's discussions and correspondence with a very wide variety of people we have been encouraged to believe that the imperatives of the Christian gospel have brought the Church to this moment of expectation. I hope that in a small but significant way, the Commission will be part of the wider prophetic voice which can prepare the Church for the next generation.

Finally, the Commission's recommendations can only be the beginning of a process and what happens next depends crucially on the spirit in which they are received.

Note

1. The report of the Commission, *Working as One Body*, is to be published in September 1995 by Church House Publishing.

Questions for Discussion

1. Give some examples of the way in which worship, service and witness are carried out at parish, diocesan and national levels.
2. Is there a viable alternative to Quota or Parish Share which would build a sense of belonging to and being responsible for the Church of England?
3. What value do you place on the development of a strategy for the Church of England?
4. How would *you* reorganize the central structures of the Church of England?

Further Reading

Colin Buchanan, *Open to Others* (Scripture Union, 1992).

Christopher Donaldson, *The New Springtime of the Church* (Canterbury Press, 1992).

Charles Handy, *The Age of Unreason* (Arrow).

Charles Handy, *The Empty Raincoat* (New York, Random House).

Charles Handy, *Waiting for the Mountain to Move* (New York, Random House).

Alister McGrath, *Evangelicalism and the Future of Christianity* (London, Hodder, 1993).

Stephen Sykes and John Booty, *The Study of Anglicanism* (London, SPCK, Philadelphia, Fortress Press, 1988).

CHAPTER FIVE

'Not One of Us'

An Exposition of Mark 9.38–41

Dick France

> [38] *John said to him, 'Teacher, we saw someone casting out demons in your name, and we tried to stop him, because he was not following us.'* [39] *But Jesus said, 'Do not stop him; for no one who does a deed of power in my name will be able soon afterward to speak evil of me.* [40] *Whoever is not against us is for us.* [41] *For truly I tell you, whoever gives you a cup of water to drink because you bear the name of Christ will by no means lose the reward.*

This obscure little story is not a favourite with preachers. It is too brief to give scope for a meaty exposition, and too enigmatic to offer a simple devotional application. But, brief and enigmatic as it is, it confronts us with an important question. How are we to regard those who appear to be on the side of Jesus and his gospel, but whom we might think of as 'not one of us'? How far, if at all, we can expect the operation of the grace of God to be confined within the recognized circles of 'the church', still less within our own approved corner of it?

This little story therefore raises important issues of ecclesiology, challenging us to think carefully about the whole concept of 'belonging'. If Jesus responded with such unexpected generosity to someone who was 'not one of us', what ought to be the attitude of those who claim to be his followers? At the beginning of the year which the United Nations has chosen to designate the 'International Year for Tolerance', this story may have a particularly timely lesson for us.

In this little narrative, the person who proposes to put a stop to the 'unauthorized' activity of the suspect exorcist is John, son of Zebedee. Mark, who has preserved this story, records elsewhere that Jesus nicknamed John and his brother James 'Boanerges', sons of thunder. In Luke's gospel, immediately after this story of the unaffiliated exorcist, we find the two of them further living up to their nickname by proposing to call down fire from heaven on the Samaritans who did not welcome Jesus and his followers (Luke 9.51–56). There, as here, their attitude earned a stern rebuke from Jesus. Perhaps their nickname derives from Jesus' embarrassment over their blunt and aggressive attitude to people outside the disciple group. They were the sort of people who see everything in black and white, to whom confrontation comes naturally; and such people can be an embarrassment to those who preach a gospel of love!

Mark tells us nothing about the suspect exorcist except that he was using the name of Jesus even though he was not, in John's view, 'one of us'. The existence of such a person should cause us no surprise: Jesus refers elsewhere to Jewish exorcists outside his own circle, with apparent approval (Matt. 12.27), and Luke's strange and vivid account of the unfortunate experience of the sons of Sceva at least illustrates that there was some potential common ground between Jewish and Christian exorcism (Acts 19.13–16). The existence of this common ground means that for Jesus and his disciples there was a choice between confrontation and co-operation. John is all for confrontation; Jesus calls instead for co-operation. He justifies his attitude by three comments.

First, 'no one who does a deed of power in my name will be able soon afterward to speak evil of me.' Whereas John favours the tighter basis of belonging which is summed up in the phrase 'following us (Jesus and his immediate circle of disciples)', Jesus operates on the more inclusive basis which recognizes support from 'fellow-travellers' even if they are not part of the 'in-group'. One who is not disposed to 'speak evil of' Jesus is to be welcomed and encouraged, not subjected to a stringent membership test.

Next comes the slogan which memorably sums up this inclusive attitude of Jesus, 'Whoever is not against us is for us'. We shall return to this generous pronouncement shortly.

Finally, Jesus speaks of the cup of water given to disciples 'because you bear the name of Christ'. It is, apparently, given by someone who again is 'not one of us', but the gift expresses a positive appreciation of what the Jesus movement stands for, and the giver will not lose his reward.

Those who are Christ's ministers in post-Christian Britain are well aware that, despite all that the Church has done to put them off, such people still exist. They may not come into our churches very often, and could make little of our theological debates, but their attitude to Jesus and even to the Church which claims to represent him is still often surprisingly positive. These are the people we have often described dismissively as 'the fringe', and our attitudes towards them have varied. There are the Boanerges among us who rather than accepting a cup of water from such people would prefer to pour buckets of cold water on their 'inadequate' religious commitment, or (to change to a more biblical metaphor) are all too quick to break the bruised reed and quench the smouldering wick. But Jesus says that these fellow-travellers will not lose their reward; they are 'not against us but for us'.

It is well known, of course, that in Matthew's gospel there is a similar saying which seems to turn this slogan on its head. In Matthew chapter 12, where the context is again one of exorcism, Jesus repudiates the Pharisees who have attributed his miracles to the power of Beelzebul with the words, 'Whoever is not with me is against me, and whoever does not gather with me scatters' (Matt. 12.30). Both formulations have in common that they exclude the middle ground: there is no neutrality in relation to the kingdom of God; you are either for or against. But what a world of difference there is in the 'feel' of the two formulae! Mark's is warm, accepting, inclusive, Matthew's harsh, rejecting, exclusive.

The reason for this is of course, at least in part, that the two contexts are fundamentally different, despite the common theme of exorcism. Those excluded by the Matthean formula are determined opponents of Jesus, whose blatantly unfounded accusation denies the manifest work of God and renders them liable to the charge of uttering the blasphemy against the Holy Spirit which can never be forgiven. The exorcist in Mark, on the other hand, is one who is co-operating in the work of deliverance, and doing it in the name of Jesus, one of whom Jesus can say that he 'will not be able to speak evil of me'. Given that there is no middle ground, it is the nature of people's response to Jesus which will determine whether they are understood to be 'insiders' or 'outsiders'; Mark's unaffiliated exorcist offers us an example of an unexpected 'insider', while Matthew's Pharisees represent clear 'outsiders', and the formula is differently framed accordingly. Luke records both incidents, and both formulae, so he at least did not see them as ultimately incompatible.

But perhaps it is not purely by chance that Matthew has simply not recorded the story of the suspect exorcist, with its inclusive formula, while Mark, who does indeed tell the story of the Beelzebul accusation, contrives to do so without mentioning Matthew's exclusive formula. Is there then perhaps also a difference in the personalities of the two evangelists, or even in their ecclesiology? Might we then suggest that in the persons of these two evangelists we can find represented in Scripture the contrasting attitudes which we find also among evangelical believers today, the exclusivists and the inclusivists, the hard-liners and the more open-hearted?

If so, this would be one of many examples of a feature of the Bible which is both one of its greatest glories and at the same time the source of much frustration for its interpreters, its ability to place side by side contrasting and even apparently incompatible elements. It is this feature of the Bible which enables evangelicals to differ over so many points of both doctrine and practice while still claiming fidelity to the scriptural revelation. If both sides of the argument are indeed validly represented in Scripture, those who claim as evangelicals to give primary weight to Scripture, and to the whole of Scripture, have no right to be dogmatic where Scripture in fact offers varying perspectives.

In practice most of us have a fairly clearly defined 'canon within the canon', consisting of those aspects of Scripture with which we feel comfortable, and in the light of which we try to reinterpret the less convenient parts. But the existence of a canon of Scripture, which embraces all this uncomfortable diversity, forbids us as evangelicals to take this easy way out, and calls on us always to recognize that the scope of biblical truth may be wider than our neat systems would allow. And where Scripture offers contrasting models, as in the case of the two formulae we have been considering, it ill behoves an evangelical to focus on the one to the exclusion of the other.

I chose to focus on the story of the suspect exorcist because it seems to me to set before us one of these contrasting emphases of Scripture which some of us may be in danger of ignoring. In our proper concern to stand firm for the truth of the gospel and to oppose views and tendencies which dishonour Christ, it is easy to adopt a 'Matthean' exclusivism which views with suspicion the more generous formula, 'Whoever is not against us is for us'. There is even a danger that we might reach the point of so priding ourselves on the integrity of our pure theological system and uncompromising pastoral policy that we write off as weak and unprincipled the more inclusive attitude which our Lord himself adopts in this story.

When I was a theological student, in the days before the ASB had been thought of, some of us were very concerned over the tendency of the Book of Common Prayer to assume that all who might require the ministrations of the church were truly members of the Body of Christ. The ecclesiology of the Prayer Book was, it seemed to us, that of a bygone age when to be English was to be a Christian, and the Church of England really did represent the nation. Surely in the latter part of the twentieth century, we would argue, we must start from the opposite perspective, and assume that no-one was a true Christian until they had proved it to our satisfaction. The parochial system, the clergyman's duty to baptize, marry and bury all comers, the principle of establishment itself, all smacked to us of compromise, of watering down the exclusive demands of the evangelical gospel.

But those who taught us were wise, and knew that the Bible contains not only Matthew's 'Whoever is not with me is against me', but also Mark's 'Whoever is not against us is for us'. So they taught us that wonderful phrase 'charitable assumption' as an expression of the pastoral strategy on which the Prayer Book services are based, and helped us to see that its ecclesiology, and therefore the ecclesiology of the Church of England, is not that of a sect but of a national Church. This was at that time the classical evangelical Anglican ecclesiology, on the basis of which evangelicals were happy to exercise their ministry within the inherited structures of the Church of England. It was an ecclesiology which often divided them from evangelicals in other denominational settings, for whom 'following us' was more narrowly defined, and the 'charitable assumption' of the Prayer Book was a regrettable historical survival. But not all evangelicals in the Church of England today seem to be as happy as their forebears with this classical position, and there are times when I wonder what has happened to the 'charitable assumption' on which our evangelical faith and ministry were nurtured.

In the story of the unaffiliated exorcist in Mark 9.38–41 we see that 'charitable assumption' writ large. I believe that our Church will be the poorer, and its impact on the nation for Christ the weaker, if it fails to include in its total outlook the conviction of Jesus himself that 'Whoever is not against us is for us'.

Questions for Discussion

1. In our own church circles, who might be seen to be in the same position as the 'unaffiliated exorcist'? Are we as welcoming towards them as Jesus was?
2. What are the limits of tolerance towards those who are 'not one of us'? On what grounds would we be justified in concluding that someone is 'not for us but against us'?
3. Are there limits to the principle of 'charitable assumption'? How does it relate to our concern for the conversion and Christian growth of those around us?

Further Reading

The following commentaries on Mark offer helpful, non-technical discussions of this passage:

L. W. Hurtado, *Mark* (New International Biblical Commentary. Peabody, MA, Hendrickson, 1983), pp. 154–55.

W. L. Lane, *Commentary on the Gospel of Mark* (New International Commentary on the New Testament. London, Marshall, Morgan & Scott, 1974), pp. 341–45.

Ched Myers, *Binding the Strong Man* (Maryknoll, NY, Orbis Books, 1990), pp. 261–62.

C. E. B. Cranfield, *The Gospel according to Saint Mark* (Cambridge Greek Testament Commentary. Cambridge University Press, 1955), pp. 309–13.

CHAPTER SIX

Jesus Christ in Today's World

Michael Nazir-Ali

We ought to be speaking of *Jesus* Christ in today's world. As ever, today also there are many claiming to be Christ and it is important to make it plain that the Christ, the Eternal Word, has *become* flesh in Jesus of Nazareth, not simply manifested himself in the flesh. In 1986 I wrote in the following way:

> Jesus Christ is the full, definitive and final revelation of God for us. Whatever else may be claimed of God, is to be judged in the light of this definitive revelation which takes place in the full light of history, though, of course, it points to that which is beyond history. The history of the man Jesus is inescapably, finally and irrevocably tied up with the Eternal Word and the one cannot be understood without the other.[1]

It is also true, of course, that the Eternal Word is not *exhausted* by the incarnation. As we often sing at Christmas time:

> The Word becomes incarnate,
> And yet remains on high.[2]

Or, as John Robinson put it: 'To believe that God is best defined by Christ is not to believe that God is confined to Christ.'[3] The Word incarnate is also the Creator and Sustainer of the universe, the one who enlightens all and in whose image we are all made. But more of this anon.

Confidence

For the moment, we need to note the importance of Jesus of Nazareth for Christian discipleship today. Wherever access to him has been denied or the possibility of knowing much about him questioned, discipleship has suffered. That is one reason why there have been so many 'quests' for the historical Jesus!

If the kerygma is to have content, we need to know at least the major events in the life of Jesus. If the kerygma, as it is preached today, is to make an impact it has to be related to 'the real and unique memory' of Jesus. In fact, *confidence* in the accounts we have of Jesus in the canonical gospels and in the rest of the New Testament is fully justified. To be sure, the gospels are not biographies in the 'detached' modern sense (if any such exist – many today either idolize or demonize their subjects!). The gospels were written by people of faith to create faith. But this is not to say that there is nothing biographical about them. Indeed, there is; they are attempting to give an ordered account of the wonderful events in the life of Jesus. The desire of the gospel writers to be faithful to the tradition which they had received is shown by the numerous instances where they have preserved the *ipsissima vox Jesu* (the very voice of Jesus) even where the early Church did not fully understand its meaning. The Son of Man sayings, for example, and the teaching about the kingdom of God are constantly on the lips of Jesus but are sparingly used in the rest of the New Testament and the sub-apostolic writings. Similarly, the *ipsissima facta Jesu*: the things he did, or his attitude which might have been embarrassing for later piety, are faithfully recorded. The cursing of the fig tree (Mark 11.12–14 and parallels), the use of spittle in the healing miracles (Mark 7.33; 8.23) and his deep emotions (Mark 1.41; Mark 11.15–18 and parallels) are all recorded.

I do not need to go into much detail here about the *quality* of the evidence: the abundance of good manuscripts in several ancient languages; the early dates of the testimonies found in Scripture (even if they are not as early as some are claiming!); their agreement with external evidence where this is available and their congruence with the *regula fidei* (the rule of faith), as it came to be articulated in the early Church. Such quality needs to be compared to the relative scarcity of good manuscripts for many classical texts and the exaggerated claims and artificiality of many apocryphal works.[4]

It is, of course, difficult to appreciate all of this if one is working with a 'reductionist' historiography which excludes the radically new from its purview, seeking only to understand the new in terms of the old, and which confines itself to the study of human beings and their relationships, refusing to allow the possibility of God acting in history. Such determinism has been effectively criticized by Pannenberg who argues for a way of understanding history which remains open to the possibility of the radically new.

In the two-thirds world and among the oppressed wherever they happen to be, liberation theology has arisen as reflection on how God's word and God's people deal with contexts of poverty, injustice and exploitation. The context often illumines aspects of Scripture, and Scripture provides the challenge and the guidance for living in particular situations in a particular way. This emphasis on discipleship has made it crucial for Latin American theologians to insist on the recoverability of Jesus. They are, of course, acutely aware of the history of biblical criticism and of all the problems it poses. They believe, nevertheless, that they cannot be satisfied with tradition mediated through 'hymns and confessions'. They seek, rather, an *ordered* account of Jesus' life, death and resurrection so that he can be *followed.* As Sobrino puts it, his *specific* humanity, with all its particularity and surprise, is the exegesis of the transcendent God.[5]

Courage

There is, of course, no turning away from a historical-critical understanding of the Bible. That way lies fundamentalism and the oppression of literalism (with which I am all too familiar in the context of another religious tradition!). We must have the *courage* to tackle the results of two hundred years of historical-critical work. While it is right, as has been indicated, to question some of its rationalist and reductionist assumptions, there can be no doubt that we are all greatly in its debt. It has, for instance, illuminated the *context* in which the life and ministry of Jesus is set. We know a great deal now about both the Jewish and the Graeco-Roman worlds which were his overlapping environs. We know much more now about some of his interlocutors such as the Pharisees and his affinities and disagreements with them.

Most importantly, perhaps, recent critical work, as Tom Wright has noted, has emphasized the *Jewishness* of Jesus: his continuity with contemporary Judaism, his attendance and activity in both Temple and Synagogue and, of course, his profound awareness of the Hebrew Bible and its authority as God's word written. At the same time, it has also highlighted *the radical challenge* which Jesus brought to Judaism: his rejection of mere ritual and custom as essential elements of religion stood within the broad prophetic tradition. But he went further, in his attitude to the Sabbath and the laws of purification, for instance. He emphasized the value of a change of heart and of the right disposition over and against the strictures of institutional religion.[6] He taught love of God and love of neighbour, even if the neighbour happened to be an enemy! In spite of his great reverence for Scripture, he was able decisively to set aside the levitical *lex talionis* (law of retaliation) in favour of his characteristic teaching on loving our enemies and praying for our persecutors. In his teaching on marriage, so impressive for people of many faiths, he regards the deuteronomic legislation as a temporary concession 'for your hardness of heart' and goes back to the creation ordinances as a more enduring basis for thinking about marriage (Mark 10. 2–12 and parallels; cf Deut. 24.1–4, Gen. 1.27, 2. 24). In the teaching, summarized for us in St Matthew's Gospel in the Sermon on the Mount, the *letter* of the Mosaic Law is repeatedly seen as minimalist and the emphasis is very much on the *spirit* behind the legislation. St Paul's remark in 2 Corinthians 3 v. 6 that the letter kills but the Spirit gives life is almost a commentary on much in the Sermon on the Mount. It was surely this memory of Jesus' attitude to the Law which enabled the early Church to declare that the legal and ceremonial requirements of the Law were not binding on Gentile converts to the Christian Faith[7] (echoed, of course, in the Thirty-nine Articles).[8]

Today also, Jesus' handling of Scripture provides a valuable hermeneutical hint. Not everything in Scripture has the same significance and not everything has the same significance for us as it might have had for past generations. Not only is Jesus Christ the exegesis of God, he is also the exegesis of Scripture. If there is a 'canon within the Canon' which can be recognized universally, it must be none other than the gospel of grace itself which is revealed in the person and work of Jesus Christ: the gospel which breaks down barriers of every kind, between God and human beings and among human beings, reconciling us with God and with our neighbours. The recognition of such a gospel will lead us to acknowledge the significance of all that in Scripture which shows us God's sovereignty and our dependence, God's holiness and our rebellion, our sinfulness and God's love, the creation of all of us in God's image and his will that we should acknowledge each other's dignity and worth.

At the same time, there *will be* aspects of Scripture that are recognized as given only for a particular people or situation or to meet a specific need. Not all of them will have immediate relevance today. We have seen already how both Jesus and the early Church set aside some of the legal and ritual requirements of the Law. Within the New Testament itself, we find that some of the prescriptions about food, agreed at the Council of Jerusalem (Acts 15), do not reappear in the rest of the New Testament. I. H. Marshall remarks in this connection that 'in the course of time the need for the prescriptions about food acceptable to Jewish Christian consciences disappeared'.[9] In the same way, it is generally recognized that some of the teaching in the so-called 'household codes' in Ephesians and Colossians (on slavery, for instance) is no longer binding on the consciences of Christians today. It is true that the Spirit will give us discernment and will lead us into all truth, but we need also to remember that the Spirit is the Spirit of Christ (Rom. 8.9). The Spirit's leading cannot be contrary to the gospel of God's reconciling love in Jesus Christ, a gospel which does away with distinctions between male and female, Jew and Greek, slave and free (Gal. 3.28).

Biblical criticism has not only enabled us to see afresh the humanity of Jesus Christ, it has also shown us again the human aspect of the Scriptures. Already, in the earliest years of the nineteenth century, many of the leaders of the Evangelical Movement had rejected plenary verbal inspiration (a phrase of Spurgeon's) as a proper basis for the authority of Scripture. They admitted, for instance, that Scripture could not be read as a scientific work (e.g. Simeon and Wilson), that there were discrepancies in the text and that some parts afforded a greater insight into the divine mind than others (e.g. Doddridge, Horne and Pye Smith). The famous Bible translator and missionary, Henry Martyn, when he was cross-examined by a Muslim court official about the nature of the Bible, replied, 'the sense is from God but the words are from the writers'.[10]

Biblical criticism's broad analysis of textual development led to a more dynamic view of revelation. Revelation was seen more and more as God dealing with his people and the world; as God active in the course of history. Scripture is the inspired and authoritative record of God's saving work, but it is also a collection of human responses to God's work among his people. These responses are subject to human limitations. They are, for example, culturally and socially determined. They have a particular world-view and a specific idiom. The hermeneutical challenge, surely, is to discover the Word of God in these contexts and to mediate it to men and women today. As Gerhard von Rad suggests in his commentary on Genesis, we need first to understand the account of creation in terms of the science and knowledge of the biblical writers *and then interpret it* to our own age in terms of contemporary science and knowledge.[11]

As far as the New Testament accounts of Jesus are concerned, we acknowledge that they have been written to meet particular needs in the early churches. We know that the writers had particular theological (and even political) motives for writing in the way they did. For instance, both R. T. France on Matthew and I. H. Marshall on Luke have shown, in different ways, the theological preoccupations of the two evangelists.[12] It is also widely recognized that one of the reasons for writing the Book of the Acts of the Apostles was to demonstrate that Christians were a legitimate religious group, a *religio licita,* within the Roman Empire and that they were loyal citizens.

We are aware that the language used by the biblical writers was often taken from the social and religious currents around them. And yet we also know that they were very careful to record all that was significant about the life of Jesus for the birth and nurture of faith. We are also aware that these accounts have been spread throughout the world, crossed many cultures and been translated into many different languages. They have brought (and still bring) millions to faith in God and in this Son, Jesus Christ. The uniqueness of Christ shines through their pages:

- the graciousness and originality of his teaching (not, of course, *de novo* originality in every case. We accept his Jewishness and his use of much in contemporary Judaism. The originality often lay in a daring new synthesis of existing elements, such as the bringing together of the two great commandments, and in the way people were challenged to make a decision).
- His ministry of healing, feeding and discipling which reveals God's love for us and his power available to us.
- His suffering and death speak to us of God who suffers with and for his creatures. They speak of the divine initiative in reconciling us to God and of divine persistence in perfecting a manifestly imperfect universe. According to Bonhoeffer, Jesus Christ condemns us for our sinfulness, judges us in our failure to measure up to God's purpose for us, but also reconciles us to God who forgives and enables us to begin anew.[13] All of these aspects are seen most clearly in the cross of Christ.
- His resurrection reveals how God can transform suffering, endured for his sake, into something glorious. It shows us how God intends humanity to be – it

> shows us our true End. It is also, of course, the basis and the explanation for the existence of the Christian Church; a people for God constituted by the memory of Jesus and experience of his risen self.

Culture and Context

This gospel has spread throughout the world and been expressed in the idiom of many different cultures. We should value each of these expressions and yet beware of absolutizing any of them. Certainly, we can learn from other ages and cultures. Indeed, our view of tradition tells us that we *must* learn from those gone before us, but we cannot simply imitate them. We should receive and express the gospel in ways best suited to our times and in language which is intelligible in our times.

But what is it that makes the gospel intelligible to people of such widely differing cultures as the Dinka of the Sudan and apartment-block dwellers in modern Seoul or Singapore? How is it that Jesus Christ makes sense in so many cultures? It is not only that there is a God-shaped hole in every human heart which the gospel can fill. It is more positive than that. It seems that there is, as Emil Brünner taught, an 'attachment-point' to God in every human being and in every human community.[14] We *are* able to respond to the divine initiative, even if it is God the Holy Spirit who makes our response possible. The image of God has been damaged but not destroyed in us. Our response to God, through his archetypal image (*eikōn* or *selem*), Jesus Christ, with the assistance of the Holy Spirit, begins the work of repair and refurbishment of the image of God in us so that we grow eventually into the stature of the fulness of Christ (Eph. 4.13).

The Word who has become flesh in Jesus Christ is also the Word who illumines every human being (John 1.9). The Word preached can be recognized by this illumination, however dim and obscure it has become because of human sin. Some years ago the World Council of Churches organized a conference on evangelism. Christians from very different ethnic, social and denominational backgrounds met to consider not only the methods and results of evangelism but also its basis. The participants agreed that the proclamation of the gospel (and its acceptance) may be seen as a fulfilment of the authentic spiritual aspirations of human kind, expressed sometimes in religious traditions but also in non-religious movements and even, at times, in *counter*-religious movements. Such proclamation may also be understood as making explicit what may already be implicit in the hearts and minds of men and women. It may be seen as bringing assurance and certainty of salvation to those who, without prior explicit knowledge of Jesus Christ as Saviour and Lord, have, nevertheless, realized their own sin and inadequacy and have thrown themselves on the mercy of God. The participants affirmed this insight of the late (and lamented) Sir Norman Anderson and saw such a state of dependence upon God as already the work of the Holy Spirit.[15] They declared that while the proclamation of the gospel will confirm and affirm certain aspects of a person's or a community's previous spiritual experience, it will judge other aspects of it. It will always be a call to repentance and new life.[16]

Much of this is true of the gospel in relation not only to the more 'exotic' of the world religions but to the more mundane realities of pastoral life in this country. The existence of folk-religion which is vaguely based on Christianity, cannot be denied. Successive studies have shown the widespread nature of implicit belief in this country and there are still civic and national manifestations of religion. Each of these provides an opportunity for an appropriate sharing of the gospel. This is not to say that we must endorse every aspect of these manifestations of religion. Far from it. We may, however, build on some aspects of these manifestations and, in the name of the gospel, challenge others.

In the *modern* age, Christians have rightly been concerned to show that Christian faith is not contrary to reason. In an age dominated by rationalism it has been necessary to establish that Christianity is credible. Our evangelical ancestors in the faith certainly did not see the Enlightenment as an unmitigated evil. David Bebbington has shown clearly that many evangelical leaders of the eighteenth and nineteenth centuries were deeply influenced by the Enlightenment on issues such as the use of the inductive method in relation to Bible Study and the Christian life generally, the equal dignity of human beings of all races and colours (which led to the campaign against slavery), personal liberty and religious tolerance. At the same time, they rejected the scepticism of many Enlightenment thinkers on matters such as divine revelation and the possibility of an immediate experience and knowledge of God.[17]

In a *postmodern* age, it may be necessary to emphasize the spirituality of Jesus, his charismatic authority and his power to restore individuals and communities to wholeness. It may be necessary to recognize that there is no one 'reason' which operates universally but that the gospel can make sense in a variety of world-views and idioms. In fact, recognition of the inescapable plurality of postmodern times may lead to the development of a variety of mission approaches. This will be true at every level of church life.

Criteria

To modify Bebbington's characteristics of evangelicals,[18] we may say that Jesus Christ will be found wherever there is *conversion*; conversion to God and to each other. Wherever people come to repent of their personal or collective wrong-doing, we may discern the work of the Holy Spirit and the illumining work of the Eternal Word who became incarnate in Jesus of Nazareth and who is the way, the truth and the life (John 14.6). Apart from him there is salvation in no one else (Acts 4.12).

We may say, then, that he will be found wherever there is *commitment*: where people recognize the demands of liberty, justice and compassion and work to have them at the very centre of their societies. Once again, there is much to learn here from the early evangelicals who struggled, with every means at their disposal, to free people from bondage, to mitigate the harshness of the economic climate around them and to bring about a change in attitudes to the poor and disadvantaged. Christ will be found wherever there is even a glimmering of the *cross*: where people know they cannot save themselves, where they look for a way back to God, where they need a Saviour to take their burdens from them, where there is suffering and oppression.

As Christians share the gospel with others while joining in with them in the struggle for justice, for instance, or as they bear the burdens of others in pastoral situations, or as the Church engages in social action, in all of these ways the unknown and implicit Christ will become known and explicit.

We cannot, however, speak only of Jesus Christ for today but also for *tomorrow*. Not only is the Word incarnate in Jesus of Nazareth, not only is he revealed today to those who seek him in a hundred thousand different ways. He is also the one who is drawing all of creation to fulfilment in himself (Eph. 1.10; Col. 1.15–20). He is 'the God before us' beckoning us to follow him. Moltmann has pointed out, however, that Christ should not be seen as simply the last term in the evolutionary process. The world, as we know it, has much waste, destruction and suffering in it. The Christ who draws all things together to fulfilment in him is one who transforms and redeems this imperfect world.[19] In him alone may we hope to find the meaning of suffering, the redemption of all that has gone wrong and the transformation of this world of waste and destruction. The resurrection of Jesus Christ from the dead is both a foretaste and a guarantee that God will bring his purposes to fruition.

Of the Father's love begotten
Ere the worlds began to be,
He is Alpha and Omega,
He the source the ending he,
Of the things that are, that have been,
And that future years shall see,
Evermore and evermore!

(Prudentius)

Notes

1. Michael Nazir-Ali, in *Towards a Theology for Inter-Faith Dialogue* (London, ACC, 1986).
2. St Germanus, 'A Great and Mighty Wonder'.
3. J. A. T. Robinson, *Truth is Two-Eyed* (London, SCM Press, 1979), p. 129.
4. See further, C. D. F. Moule, *The Birth of the New Testament* (London, A. & C. Black, 1966).
5. Jon Sobrino, *Jesus the Liberator: A Historical-Theological Reading of Jesus of Nazareth* (Tunbridge Wells, Burns and Oates, 1993), pp. 36ff; cf John 1.18.
6. N. T. Wright, *Who Was Jesus?* (London, SPCK, 1992), pp. 16, 17, 93ff.
7. Mark 7.1–23; cf. Acts 15.20, 29; Gal. 5.1–12; Col. 2.16, etc.
8. See Art. VII.
9. I. H. Marshall, *Acts* (Grand Rapids, Eerdmans, 1980), p. 254.
10. See further, D. W. Bebbington, *Evangelicalism in Modern Britain* (London, Unwin, 1989), pp. 12ff, 86ff.
11. Gerhard von Rad, *Genesis* (London, SCM Press, 1961), pp. 47ff.
12. R. T. France, *Matthew – Evangelist and Teacher* (Exeter, Paternoster Press, 1989), and I. H. Marshall, *Luke: Historian and Theologian* (Exeter, Paternoster Press, 1970).
13. D. Bonhoeffer, *Ethics* (New York, SCM Press, 1955), p. 200. See also J. V. Taylor, *The Christlike God* (London, SCM Press, 1992), pp. 256ff.

14. See further J. Macquarrie, *Twentieth Century Religious Thought* (London, SCM Press, 1971), pp. 324ff.
15. Norman Anderson, *God's Law and God's Love* (London, Collins, 1980), p. 128.
16. Stuttgart Consultation on Evangelism, 1987.
17. Bebbington, *Evangelicalism*, pp. 50ff.
18. Bebbington, *Evangelicalism*, p. 3.
19. J. Moltmann, *Jesus Christ in Today's World* (London, SCM, 1994), pp. 88ff.

Questions for Discussion

1. In what ways is Scripture God's word for you?
2. Has modern research made Jesus more real for you?
3. In what ways is the gospel making sense in your situation?
4. How do you explain 'the hope that is within you' to those who are not Christians?

Further Reading

D. W. Bebbington, *Evangelicalism in Modern Britain: A History from the 1730s to the 1980s* (London, Unwin, 1989).

N. T. Wright, *Who was Jesus?* (London, SPCK, 1992).

C. F. D. Moule, *The Birth of the New Testament* (London, A. & C. Black, 1966).

G. E. Ladd, *The New Testament and Criticism* (Grand Rapids, Eerdmans, 1967).

J. Goldingay, *Theological Diversity and the Authority of the Old Testament* (Grand Rapids, Eerdmans, 1987).

M. Nazir-Ali, *Mission and Dialogue: Proclaiming the Gospel Afresh in Every Age* (London, SPCK, 1995).

J. Sobrino, *Jesus the Liberator: A Historical-Theological Reading of Jesus of Nazareth* (Tunbridge Wells, Burns and Oates, 1993).

J. Moltmann, *Jesus Christ in Today's World* (London, SCM, 1994).

CHAPTER SEVEN

A Church *for* England

Gavin Reid

It is widely recognized that there is a morale problem in the Church of England. This is particularly felt by the clergy but it is not limited to their ranks.

The backwash from the 1992 decision to ordain women priests has proved to be more painful than was anticipated. It has opened up serious splits both on the catholic wing and amongst evangelicals. The subsequent discovery that the Church Commissioners had lost an enormous sum of money in the property slump compounded the woes. We must be under no illusions. The constant background funding of the dioceses from the Church Commissioners' earnings established a whole way of being for the Church and it is now clear that this way of being is falling rapidly apart.

The people most threatened by the funding collapse are the clergy. From now on the parishes must find the money for their stipends, and while other denominations may say that they have lived like that for generations, the fact is that they have not tried to maintain a ministry in every part of the country as has the Church of England.

These understandable occasions for morale-denting have coincided with a time when there is a low 'feel-good factor' in the country as a whole. There is a widespread dissatisfaction with the way so much of our public life is conducted. It is generally recognized that we are all living in a time of culture-shift when established ways of doing and thinking are being found wanting, and existing leadership structures are being seen to have failed. It is not a good time to be the Prime Minister and it is not a good time to be an archbishop. There is a widespread desire for scapegoats.

On top of all this there is a growing identity crisis in the Church of England. Many on the catholic wing of the Church felt that they knew who they were, where they were going and to what larger ecclesial body they belonged. The vote for women's ordination ended all those securities. Others on the evangelical side saw a way of handling the Bible being used to argue for women's ordination which they could not recognize as true to the historic evangelical position. What shook them was that many of those who they regarded as their leaders were also handling the Bible in this apparently new way. It seemed as if the rock on which they had long built their doctrinal certainties was being changed into plasticine all too easily manipulated into whatever shape was desired at the time.

This faltering sense of identity, however, has been weak for a long time. Anglican evangelicals have often felt upstaged by the more vibrant brands of evangelicalism in other denominations, and more particularly in some of the new 'house church' networks. Anglo-Catholics likewise have looked towards some future union with Rome, and the Ecumenical Movement has given rise to a sort of political correctness where one is almost expected to feel a sense of guilt for being specific about one's ecclesiastical loyalties.

When I was preparing to speak to the Westminster Conference I felt that I had to try to address this weak sense of identity. As a Scot I feel that the Church of England is very much like the people it serves. At a time when Scots, Welsh and Irish are all too clear as to their national identities, the English often feel themselves to be somewhat colourless in comparison. I think Anglicans can tend to feel the same.

My conviction is that the Church of England has a noble calling and a clear-cut identity, and the sooner that its members recover that vocation and that identity the sooner they will find their morale problems dissipating and their old and new divisions will fall into a more positive perspective.

The two questions that we need to answer are: What sort of a Church do we belong to, and what is God calling this Church to do and to be?

Alister McGrath begins his book *The Renewal of Anglicanism* by talking about a defining moment for the Church in this country.[1] That moment came in the reign of Queen Elizabeth I. She had come to the throne after one of the most dreadful periods of our country's history when Christianity had been tearing itself apart over the clash between the authority of the Catholic Church and the Bible-based teachings of the Reformers. The England she inherited was fundamentally at odds with itself; and invasion from Spain was an ever present threat. Her response was to tell the Catholic and Reformed factions to get their act together in one Church for the sake of the English people. The Church of England had to be a Church *for* England. And to do that it had to learn to *keep differences within fellowship.*

I believe that we need to reaffirm and recognize that we are *still* the Church of the original Elizabethan Settlement. A Church called to keep differences within fellowship. A Church called to treasure its catholic order and history, but also a Church that is open to the insights of the reformation, which in turn means to be ever open to further reform. That, of course, is a formula for continuous inner tension and debate. It is, by the same token, a formula for a body that can show to a divided world and a fragmented society that the grace of God can bring people who differ into a creative togetherness.

But this Church that holds difference in fellowship does not exist for its own sake. It exists to be missionary. It exists for the sake of the English peoples – whatever their views, whatever their so-called class, whatever their ethnic origins. And I believe that the only thing that can hold us together is this providential calling to exist for the sake of our country.

Of course, any true Church must, first and foremost, exist for the sake of Christ. But as St Paul once put it: 'we preach Jesus Christ as Lord, and ourselves as your servants for Jesus sake' (2 Cor. 4.5). It is not a contradiction to be centred on Christ and still to be committed to a community.

For all our faults – and they are many – and for all the evidence of more vibrant spiritual life in other quarters – and such evidence is strong – we are still the Church that is *there* for the vast majority of the peoples and communities of England. And I, for one, am unashamedly proud of that fact.

If, however, we are to be a Church for the sake of England, there are some things that we cannot be.

We cannot be a Church for the sake of the local congregation. The parish church is meant to be a church for the sake of the parish as much as a church for the sake of its congregation.

In former times the traditional village parson guaranteed this strange but vital, open, missionary relationship. By being a public figure within the community, as well as the leader of the congregation, he ensured that everyone felt that the church was *their church.* Today it is far more difficult to keep this open stance of being a church for the whole community. The steady emergence of an impersonal, TV-watching and car-owning society means that the parson is just another face in the crowd.

In a strange way also, some of the more spiritual and renewing developments can actually damage this crucial characteristic of the parish church. The great slogan of the Parish and People movement of some thirty years ago 'The Lord's service, for the Lord's people on the Lord's day' is hardly one that expresses openness to the community at large. Even charismatic renewal, to which I am personally indebted, can focus the congregation so much on its own self-expression that it develops a culture that is alien to the seeker trying to feel his or her way in.

And then, alas, there is our stuffiness. Some time ago I heard of a churchwarden who complained that the Christmas services were spoiled because they attracted young marrieds with their children!

One of the clear trends in the last twenty-five years is that our churches now carry smaller fringes. I want to ask whether people have moved away from us or whether they feel we have moved away from them? Ted Harrison, in his book *Members Only?*, quotes one incumbent as saying:

> It's not clear how long a diminishing membership and ministry in the Church of England can go on caring for the 'unchurched' who require only baptisms, weddings, and funerals. Something will have to give. I would rather spend time building up the faithful than spend it burying the 'unchurched'. I favour disestablishment because it might force folk to 'opt in' to the Anglican Church rather than just assume they are members because they are British. The Church of England will become more confessional and less communal.[2]

But there is another sense in which the Church cannot be seen to exist for the sake of the congregation. In the last twenty years or so there has been a rise in what I call 'local churchism'. Increasingly people of all traditions lionize the local congregation at the expense of the wider Church. There are good reasons for this. One of them is the need for vibrant local congregations in our increasingly impersonal and privatized world. But the parish church is only the local manifestation of something far greater. The parish church is part of the diocese which is part of the Church of England, which in turn is just a tiny part of the world-wide, history-long people of God.

The great sixteenth-century Anglican theologian, Richard Hooker argued that we needed to recognize the primacy of the universal Church and the subordinate nature of the local congregation.

> For the preservation of Christianity there is not anything more needful, than that such as are of the visible Church have mutual fellowship and society one with another. In which consideration, as the main body of the sea being one, yet within divers precincts hath divers names, so the Catholic Church is in like sort divided into a number of distinct Societies, every one of which is termed a Church within itself. In this sense the Church is always a visible society of men; not an assembly but a Society. For although the name of the Church be given unto Christian assemblies, although any multitude of Christian men congregated may be termed by the name of a Church, yet assemblies properly are rather things that belong to a Church.[3]

To over-emphasize the local congregation, and even claim that this is the main biblical dimension to the Church, is to ignore those sections in the New Testament which speak of the Church in wider terms – the royal priesthood and holy nation of 1 Peter, the Bride (not brides) of Ephesians. It fails to note that the Council of Jerusalem, in Acts 15, made decisions for and gave instructions to all the congregations of the Gentile Church. It flies in the face of the great mega-theme running through the Bible, of God seeking out a people for his own possession.

In the Church of England what that means is that congregations must take responsibility for being part of the wider Church. If we are to be a Church serving every community – to be 'there' for all the peoples of our country – there will always be fragile congregations needing the support of the stronger.

I also believe that to over-emphasize the local church is strategically disastrous in our modern, impersonal mass society. When I was the National Director of the Mission England project ten years ago, we made the impact that we did, *not* because we had Billy Graham as our main speaker, but because he gained the trust of some six thousand congregations around the British Isles so that we were focusing on the same things at the same time. That was why we could not be ignored by the media. That was why we broke into public consciousness. Unless churches pool their resources and openly work together, the name of Christ will sink without a trace in a mass media age.

To encourage today's Anglicans to bury themselves in local church activity is a formula for invisibility!

We cannot be a Church for the sake of the centralizers, be they bishops, diocesan committees or synods. I have spoken strongly about the danger of making the local congregation the main dimension of the Church – but there is a flip side to my argument. I believe that the main task of bishops and central structures is to try to provide the conditions and resources for the parish churches to flourish. It is in those congregations, and especially through the daily life and witness of their members in the community at large, that the reality of a Church for England is to be found.

I would want to resist any attempt to impose uniformed

overall strategies at the parish level. The last thing we want is some sort of 'Diocesan Curriculum' – and certainly not with testing and league tables! Each healthy church tends to develop its own individual life and style in the light of the gifts of its members and the social character of the parish. It is likely to be most effective when it is allowed to be true to itself.

One area which we are having to address in the Diocese of Canterbury is this whole business of quota. With very few large churches, and with the loss of the Church Commissioners funds, we simple cannot go on loading more and more of the cost of the smaller parishes on to the large or growing ones. That will only crush the precious life out of them. We must not be in the business of levelling down.

We cannot be a Church for the sake of the clergy. There has been a great deal of talk in the past year or so on the need to make clergy more accountable, and to end freehold. As we face the drying-up of central funds some clergy are deeply concerned for their security. We need to be very sensitive to the fears and uncertainties that are now to be found in our vicarages.

Such sensitivity, however, must not blind us to the strong clericalistic tendencies within our Church. Many people still use the phrase 'going in for the Church' when they describe someone approaching ordination. Too easily there is the misunderstanding that the clergy are 'the Church' and that the rest of us are customers or supporters of 'the Church'.

I am very cautious of talk about removing freehold. I can think of cases where a parish priest has been violently opposed from within the congregation for doing the right thing! Freehold has made it possible for faithful ministers to weather storms and carry on in ways that all have later seen to be good and beneficial. If freehold goes there will need to be clearly spelled-out safeguards.

However, there is no avoiding the fact that situations do arise where a parish priest has ceased to function properly or with conviction and where the present regulations make it virtually impossible to move the person out or on. In such a case we are crippling a congregation because we are operating as if the Church existed for the sake of the clergy. We must be able to work out some way of dealing with this without losing the proper freedoms and protections for a minister of the gospel.

Again, in the matter of appointments, we are facing changes that are not always to the liking of the clergy. Parish representatives now have far more power in the choosing of a new minister. As we move towards the day when the local congregation will be the paymaster of its clergy I can only see this trend strengthening. If the congregation pays for the priest it will want to have the major say in the choice of its priest.

All this is a far cry from the days when a bishop could move his clergy around the chess-board of his diocese. Already it is becoming more difficult for a bishop to make 'therapeutic moves' with clergy who need the refreshment of a new challenge. I am well aware that many clergy feel that all this is a retrograde development but there is some health in it. It reminds us of the importance of the local congregation. It points out that the clergy are not 'Church'. Bishops, priests and deacons are in the ministry, not the mastery.

It would, however, be wrong to end this section on a negative note. The Church of England owes an incalculable debt to its clergy. They are underpaid, under-resourced and undervalued but the vast majority of them serve their Lord and their Church with faithfulness, courage and dignity.

We cannot be a Church for the sake of its buildings. Our country has some of the most beautiful and historic churches in Europe. They are important reminders, to a generation obsessed with the present, that the Christian Faith has stood the test of time.

There is however a very big downside to this heritage. The cost of maintaining these national treasures is strangling the life of some of our village congregations and, just as serious, it actually distorts the message of Christianity. All too often the symbol of the cross is replaced by the symbol of the fund-raising thermometer.

At the heart of the gospel is the theme of grace. We are Christians because a gracious God has called us and accepted us. That God was in Christ reconciling the world to himself. Salvation is a free gift of God. When, however, Christianity is linked to monuments that have to be maintained and which the public is called upon to 'support', there is a danger that Christianity can be reduced to a cause that people are asked to patronize.

And yet there is another side to this. I am constantly moved by the actions of many non-churchgoers in our rural communities who gladly give and work for the preservation of their church buildings. I think that, in many of these cases, something deeper than patronage is taking place. Jesus told his apostles to identify where people were putting out signals of welcome and to build on those signals (Matt. 10.11). I believe that we should see those who wish to keep their church buildings as people putting out signals of welcome. The fact that they may have little desire to come into our services may say more about us than them!

We had an instance of this in one of our tiny Kentish parishes where the church building was pronounced dangerous and closed. The tiny congregation did not have the means to fund repairs but the village community took the initiative, worked hard and raised the funds. I was privileged to preach at the re-opening and found the whole community packed into the church with very obvious delight. Such times reveal that there is still a desire in many people for the 'church to be there for them'. It would be wrong to ignore this.

There is, however, the further issue of the immense amounts of money we are talking about. A recently published official Church of England poster reports – amongst many other things – that in 1992 'the Church spent £112 million on the fabric of its parish churches'. That is a tremendous sum to raise and less than 10 per cent of that came by way of English Heritage. Christian people have given very large sums of money to maintain bricks and mortar. We have to ask, in the light of Our Lord's priorities, whether this reveals that we have got things out of proportion.

We also have to question the values (if not the morality) of a government that refuses to exclude church buildings from value added tax on repairs and alterations. So the authorities with one hat on demand that we maintain these listed buildings and the authorities under another hat tax us for doing it!

There is the further question of the obligations that the authorities put upon the congregations. Most of these historic buildings are 'listed'. I cannot help feeling that if the nation 'lists' these buildings and insists upon their preservation, it must do more to pay for them.

Here we come to another part of the problem – the tension between the church building as a national monument and a place for worship and community life in the present. We have various heritage and architectural watchdogs in society today, and life would be the worse without them. However I am not convinced that the concerns of these watchdog groups take sufficiently into account the fact that church buildings are meant to be the places where the living Church expresses itself. If those bodies want to see our historic church buildings stay alive they must allow them to express the life of today and tomorrow, not be frozen as monuments to the life of some past age. As things stand, we face the real possibility of some congregations having to abandon their church buildings in order to survive.

I would like to see us being set free to think more adventurously about many of our rural church buildings. They are often the only buildings in their communities where people can gather in numbers. If we were able tastefully to adapt their interiors they could become again (as they often were in past centuries) the gathering place of both community and church, there could be great gain for congregation and parish. I am thinking of no more than carpetted naves, chairs rathers than pews, simple catering facilities and toilets. I am thinking of no more than I have already seen tastefully executed in several church buildings. It is ironic that some people feel that pews are a deeply spiritual issue, when they were later additions to the building and when many of our historic cathedrals survive without pews.

If church buildings were adapted and used more during the week, and thought of as the logical place for the community to meet, it might be all the more easy for people to cross their thresholds for worship.

We come now to four great challenges facing us if we want to be a Church for the sake of England.

First, *we face a prayer challenge.* It is perhaps significant that it was only on the day when I was supposed to address the Westminster Conference that I realized that I was preparing to talk about the great challenges facing the Church, and had excluded the place of prayer. All too often prayer becomes the last thing we think about rather than the first.

Our prayers reveal our true priorities. Privately and in public worship, intercession is important, and I dare to believe, effective. I remember hearing of a man who drifted into church one morning because he was curious and had nothing else to do. He left that church a man well on his way to conversion. The thing that had affected him most deeply was the time of intercession. It had never occurred to him that Christians cared so deeply – and believed in a God who cared so deeply – about the things that he also cared about. He said afterwards: 'By the time the vicar got into the pulpit I was ready to sign on any dotted line that he put in front of me!'

If we want to serve this country, we must pray for it. Any study of times of revival and spiritual awakening in the past has revealed that the prayers of the faithful were never very far away.

Second, *we face a cultural challenge.* If we are to be a Church *for* England we must be accessible to the differing cultures that are now part of the English scene. Make no mistake about it: England is now a multicultural country and likely to remain so.

I have only the time to touch on one consequence of this. Any future developments in liturgy will have to relate to this multicultural situation. A PCC member said to me some months ago when I was making one of my regular all-day parish visits – 'Well Bishop, we've worked hard at this, and we've had our battles, but I think we can say that we've got the worship right!' I couldn't resist replying: 'Right for whom?'

As we embark on the long process of forging a successor to the ASB, I believe that those of us in the parishes need to engage in a serious debate with the Liturgical Commission. They are a talented and skilled group of people and they know that they are there to help us. But there is some truth in the unkind saying that the difference between a liturgist and a terrorist is that you can negotiate with a terrorist! Once liturgy is in place, it is in charge.

We need a liturgy for a missionary Church – and I commend the forthcoming publication entitled *On the Way*.[4] I believe it shows a recognition of this new cultural challenge.

I don't believe that the Book of Common Prayer offers us the liturgy we need. Magnificent though it may be, it was forged in an age where every citizen was assumed to be Christian even if some were backsliding. There is only one prayer in the whole book that could be described as about evangelizing and the need for people to be converted. That is the third collect for Good Friday where we pray that 'all Jews, Turks, Infidels and Hereticks ... may be saved ...'. It is hardly a prayer that one would want to use in public worship today even if one believed, as I do, that the gospel is for all people.

The point is not that there is an offensive or inappropriate prayer in the book. The point is that the whole book is informed with that mentality in more subtle ways. Liturgy used repeatedly conveys a mentality upon its users. It is, perhaps, not surprising that some very traditional worshippers who love the Book of Common Prayer, speak as if we were still in a Christendom situation and appear to have little concern for the evangelistic task. That said, I write as a lover of the book, and I would want to see its beautiful English and clear theology kept available for the Church to use in the future.

If the Book of Common Prayer is too anchored in Christendom I feel that the Alternative Service Book goes slightly too far in the opposite direction. It is something less than the liturgy for a Church that needs to have a missionary mentality. It strikes me as a book for a congregation that is somewhat self-centred. Its overfocus upon eucharistic material reveals that it is very much a child of the 'Parish and People' mentality with its tendency to think mainly of the needs of the Lord's people set apart from the society they are called to serve.

But there is another basic problem that will need to be addressed. We have our own Church culture, and culturally Anglican liturgy is 'dinner jacket' or at least 'Sunday best' liturgy. The trouble is that we live in a leisurewear age and we need material that meets people where they are. John Drane, in his *Evangelism for a New Age*, says that the spirit of the age is a spirit of informality.[5]

There is a place for Dinner Jacket liturgy – and nobody does it better! But I believe that the England we are called to serve is, and will remain, a nation that is leisurewear and multicultural, and we need to be willing to work with very flexible liturgical tools.

Third, *we face a prophetic challenge.* We are people who read our Bibles. We have read those moving passages in Old and New Testament that speak of heaven and the new Jerusalem and the sorts of values that belong to a world filled with the knowledge of God as the waters cover the sea. If we are to bear witness to God we must bear witness to those values.

One of the things that I have discovered since becoming a bishop is that local political leaders and local media expect me and want me to talk about social and political matters. They do not want me to take sides in party political controversy, but they do look to me to bring Christian perspectives into the issues they are addressing. I have found that when I send local business and civic leaders invitations to my regular breakfast meetings where we discuss moral and spiritual matters relating to public life, the majority want to come.

I believe that there has never been a greater need for the churches to give a lead on moral and social matters. But I also believe that specifically Christian contributions need to be made in a specifically Christian way. We need to speak to the nation as members of the nation. We need to speak to the nation out of a sense of being part of the problems as much as people pointing to answers. When Nehemiah prayed about the shame of his nation, he didn't say 'they have sinned' he said, 'we have sinned'.

We also need to remember that people will look at the state of our own house before they take seriously any suggestions from us about the state of theirs. For example: one of the crying needs of our time is for the nation to take hold of a vision of being a country where people of profound differences can live positively and constructively together. Our world is racked with tribal and ethnic conflict. Britain is deeply affected by racism and class prejudice, by the rich/poor divide, and there are disturbing signs of an emerging religious bigotry – ask anyone in the Jewish community. All this provides the raw material for conflict and social upheaval.

I believe that a Church for the sake of England has an important part to play in the creation of a new, ethnically diverse, multicultural nation. But we won't have the moral authority to speak on the subject if we do not model in ourselves the ability to handle our own divisions and differences positively, inclusively and with grace. The last two years have not seen us at our best.

Again, in an age of moral uncertainty I believe that the national Church needs to demonstrate a concern for clear-cut Biblical morality – but that is not the same thing as reactionary moralizing. Biblical morality holds up the very highest standards, but it also recognizes the universal sinfulness of humanity, the need for forgiveness and the ability of God's Spirit to change us from one degree of glory to another.

Fourth, *we face an evangelistic challenge.* This is the greatest challenge of all. How are we to be a Church for England in an England that doesn't go to Church? Let me share four observations on the subject.

First – to use imagery that comes from Jesus himself – if we look out to the fields what do we see? How white are they for harvest?

I wonder how many people share with me a sense of the complexity and paradox of England as a Mission Field? We all know that our church attendance has dropped to about 10 per cent of the population – and the Church of England draws about a third of that. And yet the most recent edition of *Social Trends* lists 45 per cent of the population as claiming to be Church of England. An openness to Christianity is still widespread but interest in the institutional church is very small. And at the very time when the church attendance remains low, other forms of religious quest are taking off. According to the 1992 edition of *Social Trends* there are 30,000 Christian ministers in the UK but there are 80,000 witches and fortune tellers!

And then there is the profound ignorance of the substance of Christian faith and the contents of the Bible. I recently spoke to a group of sixth formers. Not one of them knew the story of the Good Samaritan and one asked me 'what's a clergyman?'

In our diocese, youth work is woefully weak and this is probably true of many rural dioceses. Children's work is little better, although there are some encouraging signs that people are at last waking up to the need to be more adventurous in this area. The 1989 English Churches Census found that only 14 per cent of children under fifteen are in touch with any sort of church.

The need to take children and young people far more seriously is obviously tremendously important but we must not forget that half the population is over 49 years of age. As with several other Western countries, Britain is growing older and ministry to the England of the future will have to take seriously the needs of the elderly. Spiritually, those needs can be immense. If someone has lived most of his or her life without allowing God to break in, very strong habits of rejection may have been developed.

I have only touched on a few of the many aspects of our confusing, English mission field. There are no easy answers and no single methods that will evangelize an England as complex as this, but one thing is clear. You cannot evangelize the communities and people-groups of our country from a distance or by hit-and-run tactics. You can only do it from being there in the midst of those communities. And that is where we already are.

Second, what do we mean by evangelism? Here I feel

that the Church of England, in recent years, has moved in directions that evangelicals should welcome.

Official reports such as *The Measure of Mission*[6] and *All God's Children?*[7] show that there is now a widespread recognition that evangelism is about the evangel! That may sound obvious, but I can remember being involved in theological discussions in the 1970s where such an obvious point seemed to escape detection!

What these reports are saying, and I believe they are exactly right, is that in evangelism *there is a story to tell.* People need to be helped to discover the saving significance of the story of Jesus – his birth, life, teaching, death and resurrection. Evangelism has to be biblical.

Thirty years ago evangelistic preachers could start by assuming that people already knew the story. Today evangelists have to assume that their hearers do not know the story. We are back to true evangelizing – helping people to discover the gospel.

But one thing that concerns me is that you cannot really see the good news of Jesus unless you also see the bad news of trying to live without him. We must face the realities of sin and judgement. And here I feel that there has been a reluctance in the Decade of Evangelism to grasp this nettle. We are terrified of offending or appearing to be hellfire cranks. The truth is, however, that the gospel is not about life enhancement – *it is about lost people finding salvation.*

Third, how do we get this story over? Another one of the positive developments in the last few years is the widespread recognition that *people usually respond to the Gospel slowly.* Sudden conversions are not the norm and never were. This means that we need to move away from understandings of evangelism that focus on the need to produce sudden conversions in people's lives, towards an evangelism where we think of resourcing the process of discovery in people's lives.

Research by people like John Finney[8] has shown that

this gentle opening up to faith, which is what happens with most Christians, is usually the consequence of being in contact with people who already have faith in Christ. As some put it, and helpfully, *belonging usually comes before believing.*

The old assumption on which much evangelical evangelism was based, was that people should be brought to belief, and then you tried to get them into a Christian church where they could experience belonging. This view spawned an over-reliance on words as opposed to relationships. What we now see clearly is the need for relationships without denying that words matter. The response to the gospel itself often follows a response to the people of the gospel. Writers like William Abraham in his book *The Logic of Evangelism* rightly point out that the line between evangelism and nurture is a pretty blurred one.[9]

What all this boils down to is the need for our churches to be as 'outsider-friendly' as possible in the range of services and other activities offered. I am concerned that over the last thirty years the percentage of confirmed people in the population has plummeted at the very time when the proportion of Eucharists offered as the main or only Sunday service has rocketed. It makes me wonder whether we are serious about being parish churches.

What we urgently need to do is to create contexts where belonging can be experienced by people who are not yet ready for commitment, and where teaching and explaining can be carried out in this atmosphere of belonging. The growing success of such approaches as Alpha Groups does not surprise me.

I come to my fourth and final point. What about the future? And here I return to the analogy of farming and the harvest. I once heard it said that a good farmer did not just think about this year's harvest. He also thought about what was needed to ensure a good harvest next year.

This is where I feel we have been failing. Our evangelistic strategies – when we have any – have been too shortsighted. This is also why I feel that we need to give a far higher priority to work amongst children. We need to start with the way we deal with baptism inquiries and move on through the provision of playgroups and parents and toddlers activities. We need weeknight informal children's clubs. We need to stay in church schools. We have to make a serious attempt to draw as many children as possible into an experience of belonging to a Christian peer group where the story is told. I do not think we will ever again have effective youth work until it can be built on the solid base of energetic children's ministry. I am convinced that we have two main tasks in evangelism. To share the faith with our own generation and to keep the faith for the next generation.

The older I get, the more I see that I am a Christian because people down the centuries have passed on the faith from one generation to another. Now it is our turn. You and I have been entrusted with the gospel by a God who measures time in centuries rather than seconds. That is why the future spiritual health of our country must matter to us. That is why we need to work away at keeping faith linked into the institutions of our national life. That is why – with all the flexibility I call for – we still need liturgical passages that will lock themselves into the memories of as many people as possible. It is why we simply must, for example, bend every effort to ensure that the new millennium opens with only one version of the Lord's Prayer in use in every context throughout society.

I close with a verse from Plumptre's famous hymn 'One Church, one Faith one Lord'. In the early verses of the hymn, Plumptre tells how God's hand has guided the Church from age to age in its task of holding and passing on the faith. The fifth verse brings us to the present and puts the present generation on the spot.

> And we, shall we be faithless?
> Shall hearts fail, hands hang down?

Shall we evade the conflict
And cast away our crown?
Not so; in God's deep counsels
Some better thing is stored ...
We will maintain, unflinching
one Church, one Faith, One Lord.

May God help us to do just that!

Notes

1. Alister McGrath, *The Renewal of Anglicanism* (London, SPCK, 1993), p. 12.
2. Ted Harrison, *Members Only?* (London, Triangle, 1994), p. 11.
3. Richard Hooker, *Laws of Ecclesiastical Polity*, Book III.i. 14, cited by H. Bettenson, *Documents of the Christian Church* (London, OUP, 1943), pp. 412f.
4. *On the Way: Towards an Integrated Approach to Christian Initiation* (London, Church House Publishing, 1995).
5. John Drane, *Evangelism for a New Age* (London, Marshall Pickering, 1994), p. 49.
6. *The Measure of Mission*, General Synod Document 780A (London, Church House Publishing, 1987).
7. *All God's Children?* Report of General Synod Board of Education and Board of Mission (London, National Society and Church House Publishing, 1991).
8. John Finney, *Finding Faith Today* (London, Bible Society, 1992).
9. William Abraham, *The Logic of Evangelism* (London, Hodder & Stoughton, 1989), chap. 6.

Questions for Discussion

1. Do you agree that England is becoming both multicultural and 'leisurewear'? Are there not some clear-cut cultures in our country (e.g. the Afro-Caribbean groups) who, as well as the elderly, are more formal, particularly with regard to 'church'? How would you modify the comments made in this article in relation to such groups?

2. Do you think £112 million is too high a figure to pay in one year for the maintenance of parish churches? How do we judge whether money should be spent on buildings or not?
3. How much part was played by 'coming to believe' and 'coming to belong' in your personal story of Christian beginnings and conversion?

Further Reading

Robert Warren, *Building Missionary Congregations* (London, Church House Publishing, 1995).

All God's Children? – Children's Evangelism in Crisis (London, Church House Publishing, 1991.)

David J. Bosch, *Transforming Mission* (Maryknoll, NY, Orbis, 1991).

CHAPTER EIGHT

A Gospel for Our Culture

Graham Cray

My contribution is to develop Bishop Gavin's emphasis on the cultural context of our mission as a 'Church for the sake of England'. Cultural analysis and the relationship of mission to culture are complex issues and inevitably I am only able to give the starkest outline in the space available. But at least I can provide an agenda for further study and place some internal evangelical disputes into a broader context.

The basic principles of the relation between gospel and culture are clear. First, the gospel itself does not change. Its central message of salvation through the work of Christ is for every age and culture, although it has to be 'proclaimed afresh' within each generation. This is reflected in the formularies of the Church of England. Whatever anyone may say to the contrary, the Church of England is a confessional Church; not in the sense of having primary confessions of faith which distinguish it from other denominations, but in the sense that its Canon law, the Book of Common Prayer, the Ordinal and the Thirty-nine

Articles of Religion all recognize the authority of the historic creeds precisely because of their scriptural basis. Our Church is committed to Scripture, to the credal statements in which the ancient Church recognized the scriptural gospel, and to its own historic formularies because they also express that gospel. On this credal basis evangelical Anglicans recognize the Church of England as their theological home.

But second, culture does change; so the way in which we express the gospel must also be open to appropriate change if it is to be proclaimed afresh in each generation. This is not the same as accommodating the gospel to the spirit of the age, although no generation of Christians can avoid facing that possibility.

Much of the urgency behind my own study of contemporary culture has been motivated by a different possibility. A quotation from John V. Taylor puts it most clearly. 'When my son decided to give up on the Church, he said to me, "Father, that man [the preacher] is saying all of the right things, but he isn't saying them *to* anybody. He doesn't know where I am and it would never occur to him to ask!"'[1] My fear for evangelicals is that we say all the right things (the unchanging gospel) but we do not say them to anybody because we do not know how much our culture has changed or how far out it has moved. It is true that in our anxiety to be heard we might accommodate the gospel but that is no excuse for failing to try to communicate.

Crucial to this whole exercise is our handling of Scripture. In recent correspondence John Stott has spoken of

> a difference between cultural transposition (which affirms the essence of the biblical revelation while retaining the liberty to change its cultural expression) and a kind of cultural rejection, which claims the liberty to set aside any biblical teaching on the grounds that it is culturally antiquated.

A clear example can be given in the doctrine of the atonement.

Evangelicals will first ask what the Bible teaches about the cross. The considered answer to that question will then be set over against all interpretations and traditions, even evangelical ones. When, for example, some evangelical scholars suggest that Paul's understanding of the death of Christ does not necessarily include the idea of retribution, we may or may not agree; but the determination to establish the original meaning of the text and the intention of the author is central to the evangelical tradition. We are committed to *semper reformanda*, the continual reform of our own traditions in the light of Scripture.

But we are also committed to evangelism and apologetics. So we ask how the truth of an objective atonement is to be communicated. We recognize that different metaphors have been emphasized in different cultural eras: 'ransom' in the patristic period, 'satisfaction' in the medieval, 'penalty for breaking the law' at the time of the Reformation, 'example' in the Enlightenment era. Each of these needs testing by Scripture and on that basis some are more adequate and complete than others, but the exercise is essentially sound. It is right to express the message of the cross in the categories of our day, as long as those categories do not distort the biblical meaning. So recently, in his book *The Cross of Jesus*, Leon Morris explored biblical dimensions of the atonement which he saw as particularly telling in contemporary culture.[2]

This challenge to interpret the gospel *both* faithfully *and* appropriately has always been the Church's task, but at this particular time we face an additional substantial complication, namely, *we live at the time when Western culture is shifting from the modern to a postmodern era.*

Ours is a time when the cultural era which has transformed the world out of all recognition, for good and ill, is coming to an end. Western culture was based on and developed from the thinking of the eighteenth-century

Enlightenment. The great strength of Enlightenment thinking was that it freed the quest for knowledge from the constraints of imposed tradition and opened the way for contemporary scientific enquiry. In this it assumed the consistency and therefore investigability of the universe; a belief rooted in the Christian doctrine of creation. At the same time however it secularized the Christian doctrine of providence into the ideology of 'progress', and enthroned human detached reason as the final authority, relegating both revelation and spirituality to the private sphere of personal opinion and values. It is this underlying world view that has collapsed, creating a very different context for mission and evangelism.

In overall terms the new context is neither better nor worse than its predecessor, *but it is different*! Just as it is not possible to evaluate the Enlightenment in the terms of *1066 And All That* as either 'a good thing' or 'a bad thing', so the new mission context has gain and loss for the Church's mission, as well as genuine continuities. The breakdown of confidence in the omniscience of detached reason reopens a door that was bolted against us. But the new incredulity towards *any* overall frameworks of truth confronts us with a substantial new problem. It is one thing to put the power of human reason back into proper perspective, it is quite another to relativize it altogether.

We are now in a time of transition called by many post-modern. This is a slippery term used by many to name the cultural era which they see as replacing the Enlighten-ment or 'modern' one. However the term is best under-stood not as describing a new culture, but as a recognition that something has ended, and that we do not yet know what will take its place. Any movement which describes itself as 'post' what went before does not yet know what it is! The term has a semi-popular use to describe the sense of uncertainty and ambivalence resulting from this transi-tion.[3] In the words of the Chief Rabbi, 'We are caught between two ages, one passing, the other not yet born.'[4]

This is a time when secular certainties are as much under question as sacred ones; and when there is more certainty about what we can no longer believe than what we can believe instead.

- Instead of objective truth established by human reason, many people feel they can only be sure of what they subjectively feel.
- Instead of an ideological certainty about human progress and a better future, there is uncertainty and sometimes cynicism about the future.
- Instead of the self-confidence of human beings who regard themselves as in essence autonomous individuals, there is a crisis over human identity and lasting relationships.

This collapse of the Enlightenment world view gives the Church major new opportunities.

There is a spiritual thirst and quest in our nation beyond anything in our lifetimes. Prayer and meditation courses, New Age networks, an interest in Eastern religions and pre-Christian nature paganism all testify to the fact that many people can no longer live without an overtly spiritual dimension to their lives. Our technological and bureaucratic society has been brilliant at answering 'How?' questions, but incapable of answering 'Why?' questions. And as Lesslie Newbigin has said 'The human spirit cannot live permanently with a form of rationality that has no answer to the question "Why?".'[5] The split between public and private spheres, derived from the philosophy of John Locke, in which religion was confined to the private sphere, is breaking down. Spirituality is re-invading the public square, but any and every spirituality; and there are no universally recognized maps!

The new openness to spirituality provides us with an opportunity but no guarantees. Indeed, if people have any opinions about Christianity at all, it is often regarded as the last place to look for spiritual reality. We Christians may see ourselves as the defenders of spiritual truth *against* Enlightenment rationalism, but in many peoples' eyes we are part of a passing and failed age: a religion which did nothing to prevent the various crises the West now faces. To some, the Church is a clear example of a failed hierarchical organization well past its sell-by date.

What we now face is not so much secularism and rationalism as the challenges of a pluralist and relativist society. We are called to bear witness to Christ in a culture suspicious that claims to truth are no more than power plays. Christendom is dead. The gospel has to be proclaimed in a culture where, as in the New Testament, it is one voice among many, with no special privileges.

Despite the revival of interest in spirituality, many people are simply numbed by the affluence of a materialist society. They no longer believe that the past has anything significant to tell them, and they have lost their ideological certainty about a better future. So they live for the present, not because they are more selfish than those who have gone before, but because there does not seem to be a viable alternative. We still enjoy a lifestyle born of the Enlightenment, even though the intellectual foundations that produced it have collapsed. Simultaneously we doubt and put our faith in the technological society. For many people that is enough. A life of shopping and viewing and feelings for feelings sake acts as a kind of anaesthetic. This is the contemporary way in which 'the god of this world has blinded the minds of the unbelievers, to keep them from seeing the light of the glory of the gospel of Christ' (2 Cor. 4.4).

Far too many people are content to 'enjoy the surface' of postmodern culture, but just beneath the surface are questions which will not go away, and to which the gospel of Christ, biblically proclaimed, has profound answers. We will focus on three.

1. *How can I know what is true beyond what I feel?* Hermeneutics is the disturbing issue for the whole

Western world, not just for evangelicals. This culture implies that no claim to truth has any more authority than any other; that truth is no more than what an individual makes of life, or at best what a local culture is evolving. Some see this as a liberation, others stoically accept what they regard as inevitable; but there is something in the human person, created in the image of God which knows that truth is more than this and that without it society can only fragment. The second question follows on directly.

2. *How can relationships be sustained and community restored?* The breakdown of marriage and the family, the destruction of community and the loneliness of people crowded together in urban areas is a self-evident crisis of our day. It is also the most accessible point of contact for the local church's mission. It is the direct consequence of Enlightenment individualism; of the belief that human fulfilment is found in being freed *from* the claims of others rather than freed by Christ *for* the service of others. On the basis of their own painful experience many people want to know how human beings can find some way to live together in mutuality, sacrifice and respect? The third question adds a further relationship.
3. *How can we relate in a different and better way to the earth?* Many readers who have school age children and who are not recycling their household waste, will have had their children wanting to know why not. It is a self-evident matter to many younger members of the population that our environment is in desperate trouble as a result of our lifestyle choices. Yet there is much more awareness of the relationship between Western lifestyles and environmental needs than there is spiritual strength and moral vision to change our way of life. In the postmodern era a proclamation of the gospel

> which relates redemption to the future of creation is essential.

Our society needs a new world view to answer its unanswered questions and in its disillusion with the answers provided by the Enlightenment it has lost its hope of finding any further integrating framework of truth. Zygmunt Bauman, one of the leading sociological commentators on postmodernity expresses very clearly this loss of trust in society's 'moral voices'.

> In a cacophony of moral voices, none of which is likely to silence the others, individuals are thrown back on their own subjectivity as the only ultimate ethical authority. At the same time however they are told repeatedly about the irreparable relativism of any moral code. . . . There are no obvious social agencies that may guide the choice between indifference and solidarity.[6]

This is the challenge to the Western Church at the close of the twentieth century. 'No obvious social agencies'? I know of one. If it can have the courage and the humility to engage with these questions with sufficient seriousness.

But the Church is not a detached source of answers to the Western world's problems. Although its identity is rooted in a different place, it is also part of the culture which is collapsing. It is itself struggling with the same questions. Just as our Lord Jesus could not be a universal 'everyman' but had to be a Jew of the first century, so the Church can only take its form within a particular culture. In our case the Enlightenment based culture of the West. It is not 'their' culture which is collapsing, but ours also. The culture in which we were shaped and educated, which has formed us far more than we know, and in which we have attempted to be faithful to Christ.

All parties in the Church of England are to some extent children of the Enlightenment. All are suffering the same identity crisis. The Liberal tradition more than any other, because it is more directly the child of the Enlightenment than any other. Newbigin summarizes the consequences. 'It seems that those religious bodies which have tried to accommodate as much as possible of the rationalism of the Enlightenment are in decline, and that those which have maintained a strong emphasis on the supernatural dimension of religion have flourished.'[7]

But evangelicalism as we now know it took its form both in reaction to the Enlightenment, and as a child of the Enlightenment.[8] The Evangelical Revival was the biblical antidote to deism. But the clarity of the message of Wesley, Whitfield and their peers was made possible by the emphases of the Enlightenment. A new confidence in the reliability of sense experience allowed our forefathers to understand the scriptural teaching on assurance in a way that had partly eluded previous generations. The new certainty of the assurance of salvation was the mainspring of the Evangelical missionary movement at home and overseas. Culture shift can throw new light on what is objectively in the Scriptures, but was previously veiled by culture, just as much as it can profoundly distort our ability to see things that once we saw clearly.

As the era which shaped us comes to an end, our evangelical identity crisis should be understood as part of a much wider shift in confidence and in thought. It is pointless to blame one another. We need to engage these issues together for the sake of the gospel, and of effective communication of the gospel to the nation.

Group identity and boundaries are very difficult to maintain at such a time. Things we have taken for granted seem no longer to be taken for granted; especially as we find ourselves disagreeing over the interpretation of Scripture in the light of new issues such as the ordination of women. But in a time of cultural transition it is genuinely difficult to discern the boundaries between essentials of the biblical faith and the way we have always done things as far as we can remember. It is not difficult to discern the core of the gospel. The uniqueness of Christ, for instance, comes into clearer focus in a pluralist culture. But we should not be surprised to find substantial boundary disputes among us at the moment. The challenge we face is cultural appropriateness without syncretism.

Resources for the Transition

Our tradition provides us with adequate resources for the task. As ever, Scripture is the touchstone against which everything else must be tested. Not only as to the content of the gospel but also as the primary resource for engaging with cultural transition. In the Old Testament, Jeremiah was the prophet to a culture that was dying but believed itself to be indestructible. In this it anticipated the culture of the West which has been so convinced of its scientific objectivity that it has thought itself immune from the fate of all previous cultures, yet alone the judgement of God!

In the New Testament, the transition from a Jewish mission to a predominantly Gentile one provides the background or foreground to most of the early Church's internal disputes. As scripture people we should not be surprised at intense mutual disagreements when those raised to communicate the gospel in one cultural environment find themselves in a new one. We have much to learn from the Jewish New Testament missionaries who were called to proclaim Christ in a Gentile culture and who struggled to distinguish which parts of their theological upbringing were central to the gospel and which were culturally relative.

Because of our primary commitment to Scripture, it is particularly painful for us when many of our disputes are focused on hermeneutics. Interpretation of truth becomes particularly difficult when the cultural furniture is moving round. We cannot simply repeat the arguments which were used most effectively to battle Enlightenment rationalism. Theologians of Scripture like Benjamin Warfield used the thought forms of their day to present the truth that Scripture is God's authoritative word written. Scripture is indeed God's word written, but the lines of argument will necessarily be different today. Warfield shared with his opponents some assumptions about the nature of truth which are now under question and which are not essential foundations for the defence of Scripture. As we engage with a different theory of knowledge we need different arguments. However the clear consensus of all our evangelical forefathers that Scripture reveals and rightly interprets God's saving action in history through Christ is not negotiable. Regarding hermeneutics, however much postmodern culture may understand truth as any meaning the readers establish to their own satisfaction, an evangelical hermeneutic starts with the assumption that the text conveys a truth which encounters and makes claims on its reader, and which therefore radically limits the possible alternative interpretations. Within these boundaries we can retain the best insights of our past and address the questions of our day. We must not abandon our predecessors' apologetic concerns, nor can we repeat them whole. New answers are required to new questions.

We have no need to panic – culture shifts like this have happened before – but we do need to trust the Holy Spirit. David Bosch, in his book 'Transforming Mission',[9] describes how the mission of the Church has had to adapt as culture changed from era to era. We need to look back at those other culture shifts.

Evangelicalism found its present form in the eighteenth century, but its theological roots are in the Reformation. A re-examination of our Reformation heritage will help us distinguish those aspects of evangelical culture which have been both secondary and specific to the Enlightenment era.

The Evangelical Revival itself was an outpouring of the Holy Spirit; God's answer to reductionist Enlightenment rationalism. We need to pray again for such an outpouring. The Christian gospel is not just historical and objective truth; it is not just public truth with the power to shape a culture; by God's mercy it is transforming truth! We need a church alive in the power of the Spirit to proclaim it. This century's Pentecostal and Charismatic movements (including the 'Toronto Blessing') need to be assessed from this perspective. Jim Packer has written

> What shall we say of the world-wide charismatic movement of the past thirty years? Laying aside matters of detail, I believe that God has generated it in order to counter the death-dealing fashions of thought and theology which, starting with theologians and spreading everywhere, for the past century have done damage by demurring at the truth of the Trinity, diminishing the deity of Jesus Christ, and for practical purposes discounting the Holy Spirit altogether.[10]

This is a time when those evangelicals who emphasize the teaching ministry and those who emphasize the ministry of the Spirit need one another. The Word cannot be used to protect the Church from facing today's questions (which it is more than capable of answering), nor dare we treat experiences of the Spirit as automatically self-authenticating and as an end in themselves.

Finally, we need to learn from the second century when there was tension between the views of theologians like Tertullian, who saw their whole culture as demonic and as offering no grounds for compromise without accommodation, and those apologists like Justin Martyr and Clement of Alexandria who claimed to find bridges into their culture without accommodation. Those who are concerned that we might be accommodating the gospel, and those who are battling to speak the gospel into this culture need one another; or we could end up with one half of evangelicalism culturally marooned and the other half no longer distinguishable as Christian.

Today there is an urgent need to maintain dialogue within the evangelical movement. We need to face new questions without abandoning scriptural insights. It is also urgent to maintain dialogue with the other Christian traditions who also have to engage with the same questions.

Conclusion

The challenges we face are not just matters for our own generation. Because we are called to serve Christ during a shift in cultural eras, we are laying foundations that, if our Lord does not return, will be built on by many future generations of believers, for better or for worse. Culture is the double challenge we face; how to interpret the Bible to our culture *and* how to understand the place of culture in interpreting the Bible. Both issues must be tackled if the Church of England is to be the Church for England in the postmodern era.

Notes

1. J. V. Taylor, lecture at School of World Mission, Fuller Seminary, 1971, quoted in Charles Kraft, *Christianity in Culture* (Maryknoll, NY, Orbis, 1979), p. 279.
2. Leon Morris, *The Cross of Jesus* (Grand Rapids, Eerdmans; Exeter, Paternoster Press, 1988).
3. For the best outline of the debate about the postmodern, see David Lyon, *Postmodernity* (Open University, 1994).
4. Jonathan Sachs, *The Persistence of Faith* (London, Weidenfeld, 1991), p. 20.
5. Lesslie Newbigin, *The Gospel in a Pluralist Society* (London, SPCK, 1989), p. 213.
6. Zygmunt Bauman, *Intimations of Postmodernity* (London, Routledge,1992), page xviif.
7. Newbigin, *The Gospel*, p. 213.

8. See D. W. Bebbington, 'Evangelical Christianity and the Enlightenment', in M. Eden and D. F. Wells (eds.), *The Gospel in the Modern World* (Leicester, IVP, 1991).
9. David Bosch, *Transforming Mission* (Maryknoll, NY, Orbis, 1991).
10. J. I. Packer, *A Passion for Holiness* (Leicester, Crossway, 1994), p 62f.

Questions for Discussion

1. To what extent do you recognize the changes in culture described in this chapter?
2. In what way has your church been influenced by these changes?
3. What are the best 'bridges for the gospel' into today's culture?
4. In what ways do evangelical disagreements echo the change in culture?
5. What are the most significant aspects of the evangelical doctrine of Scripture in the light of today's issues?

Further Reading

Graham Cray, *The Gospel and Tomorrow's Culture* (CPAS Wordbook, 1994).

Lawrence Osborne, *Restoring the Vision* (London, Mowbray, 1994).

Martin Robinson, *The Faith of the Unbeliever* (Tunbridge Wells, Monarch, 1994).

Gene Veith, *Guide to Contemporary Culture* (Leicester, Crossway, 1994).

CHAPTER NINE

Holding On and Holding Out

Philip Hacking

Hold On and Hold Out

I will begin with two Scripture texts which for many reasons have haunted me over the past few months in my own local church ministry and in the wider work to which I have somewhat reluctantly been drawn as chairman of *Reform.* One of the verses is in Philippians 2.15f where Paul reminds us that we are 'to shine like stars in the universe holding out', or you can translate it 'holding on to the words of life'. That comes after the great passage of our Lord's servanthood, our Lord's obedience to grace and truth.[1] In response to that we are to reflect him not just in servanthood, though that is very important, but holding out and holding on to the words of life. Scripture reminds us that we are to reflect our Lord and thereby make God real to our generation. John puts it succinctly when in his gospel (1.18) he begins by reminding us that nobody has ever seen God, and then goes on to point out that the only Son has made him known. In 1 John 4.12 he begins exactly the same way but then points out that if we love one another God lives in us. The challenge cannot ever be ducked by evangelical Christians.

I believe we need to be reminded of our need to recognize the desperate dying state of those who are lost. I am glad that Gavin Reid reminded us of the lostness of the lost, the deadness of our world (chapter 7). Words of life only matter because people out there are dying and I hope we shall not be so triumphalist that we forget that. Moreover, we need confidence that what we have in our hands is the word of life and that we have the privilege of taking out that word of life, holding on to it and holding it out.

The second text is that well-known verse from 2 Timothy 2.2 which we cannot forget. Over history that has been a great blessing to many Christians: 'The things you heard me say in the presence of many witnesses entrust to reliable men who will also be qualified to teach others.' Paul is handing on to Timothy a tremendously important deposit. He talks in chapter 1 about the good deposit to be guarded, the pattern of sound teaching. If we read on in 2 Timothy 2, Paul refers with absolute conviction to what he calls 'my gospel'. That is not a suggestion that it is one of many varieties. In our relativistic age, how popular it is that you can take your pick. Paul insists that *my* gospel is the gospel. Indeed elsewhere he will point out that if we preach any other, even if an angel from heaven, however beautifully he may do it, let him be accursed, let him be eternally condemned. Read further in 2 Timothy 2, where God's word is not chained, but Paul is chained and he is suffering for the sake of the elect. Some of us have been through a certain amount of suffering over recent months and years and I guess that may be true for many of us, suffering within the body of evangelicalism within the Church of England.

I have been pondering on what grounds I was asked to make a contribution to the Conference. I hope it was because I am basically a parish minister. I have spent ten years as an Englishman in Scotland and the last twenty-six as a Lancashireman in Yorkshire, so at least courage is one of my prerogatives. I have been a parish minister for a long time and God has been gracious and blessed. I have been involved in evangelism in the Church in England and also in Northern Ireland, Scotland and Wales. I believe that it is also because I am Chairman of *Reform* which I unashamedly represent as well as contributing in my own right. I do believe God has called us to say something important today. *Reform* is barely two years old, a ginger group born out of the turmoil over the ordination of women, but with many other deep concerns as outlined in our Covenant signed by hundreds of clergy and laity. We do believe that we were called to make our representation and I am happy that I am able briefly to speak today.

Anglican Evangelical

I hope also I have been invited to contribute because I am quite openly evangelical first and an Anglican second. My kinship is with all who love the gospel. I do not find an equal kinship with those who happen to be in the same denomination but deny the gospel. I am an Anglican, I have been reared as one, I was converted in an Anglican church and I hope to end my days serving the Lord within the Church of England, which is very precious. But my main roots are evangelical and with that in mind I want to point out two things in Philippians 2. We are to *hold on* and we are to *hold out*. That is, if we are going to be effective in evangelism then we need to be confident about the evangel.

Holding On

The Person of Jesus

His uniqueness depends upon the truth, the absolute

sovereign truth of Scripture and that is here in God's final word to men and women. Yes, it must be interpreted in our day, but we are not, as it were, hoping that there may be more truth. We are shut in to the Word of God. I was taught by a great man called Alan Stibbs to whom many others owe a tremendous amount. One of his great verses was 'Let God be true and every man a liar' (Romans 3.4). Stand by the truth whatever it may cost. While it is true that in our age we must speak to our culture, some of us are concerned that culture begins to decide what we preach. There is the apostle Paul preaching at Athens. Of course he understood the Athenian culture, he quoted a poet of theirs, he started from one of their inscriptions but he also preached about repentance, judgement and Jesus and the resurrection. There was no accommodation. (Acts 17.16–34)

Human Sexuality

Some time ago, an Anglican vicar was speaking at the Keswick Convention, where I have been involved for so many years, and he reminded us that there are two ways of demolishing a building. You may put some Semtex there and blow it up in one fell swoop or you may go down to the basement every lunch-hour and remove a brick here and a brick there, and eventually it will collapse. Some of us feel that in the Church of England people have been removing bricks. There are a number of us who did feel unhappy about the decision over the ordination of women on the headship matter of biblical principle[2] and we were concerned that evangelical bishops, I think with one exception, did not vote the way we felt Scripture suggested they should have voted. We have therefore started *Reform*. We are still concerned about the dangers of marginalization, and there are young people here, as well as older people, who fear about their future because of what we believe to be clear biblical teaching. We are now concerned, in relation to homosexuality, that we are in danger of not being as clear on biblical principles there as we should be. My hope is that not only shall we not see clergy being allowed to live in a homosexual relationship, but that the prohibition will extend to laity. We did ask our evangelical bishops to distance themselves from some unbiblical statements in the House of Bishops Report *Issues in Human Sexuality*[3] and we still await a reply. The forces against us are strong and determined and we need the courage to stand up and be counted. We find it difficult to believe that you can have two standards of morality. We see this as an inroad into Scripture and ask where it is all going to end. It all depends on our confidence in the word of God.

Multi-Faith

Surely that is true also about the person of Jesus whose uniqueness is as the only Saviour. We are all unique, you are unique, I am unique. There will be nobody again like you or me, but Jesus Christ was unique as the only Saviour. We find that being eroded by multi-faith worship. We do believe it is right to communicate lovingly, tolerantly and carefully with those of other faiths. But we do believe it is right, for example, that Jews should be led to faith in Jesus Christ and that we should say unashamedly that there is a gospel that should lead them to faith in Jesus. The uniqueness of Christ still stands or falls by the unique authority of Scripture. In this International Year of Tolerance, while we should support every attempt to fight against the evil of racism, we must dare to be thought intolerant as we refuse to diminish the person of Christ or the truth of Scripture.

Moral Integrity

We believe that holding on to the truth means moral integrity in leadership. Yes, we are all sinners, we all come needing forgiveness, but I do not believe that the world will listen to us, that England will listen to us, unless they see integrity in leadership and that we stand by Christian moral standards at all costs. This involves many aspects of morality, including very clear teaching against materialism and greed, which we must not ignore. But Scripture does identify sexual sins as a special danger and many of the lists in the New Testament of the things that offend God are headed by sexual sins.

The Local Church

Holding on, I believe, is to take the scriptural view of the church, both local and universal. I do not believe, however much we try to manipulate it, that we can find the Church of England within the Scriptures. I am happy enough that we can be Anglicans and true to the New Testament. But surely in the New Testament the Church is the local church and the universal Church. Yes, we must be careful not so to emphasize the local church that we miss our responsibility to the wider community of the people of God. But I am concerned that all too often what is happening in the Church of England has taken away the freedom of the local church, and here I believe is where evangelism essentially begins. It is the heart of our evangelistic ministry. What holds us together is not episcopacy but the truth of Scripture. The focal point of unity is not the bishop but the Bible. We must accept the rightful authority within our denomination, but evangelicals have always seen episcopacy as not being necessary to the Church, although a fitting way of government. However, it is one which needs radical rethinking in our age. I believe it is vital that we affirm that we do stand by evangelical truth. Perhaps I am naive, I had always believed that the Church of England was basically an evangelical body and that what we believe in – the doctrine of the Church of England – is evangelical truth. Unashamedly we hold on to it. Watch the danger of erosion.

Hold Out

Evangelicalism Leads to Evangelism

I am glad that Gavin Reid has pointed out that evangelism is basically confidence in the evangel. In all the missions I take up and down the country I simply seek to expound the truth wherever I am, allowing for cultural differences. One of the greatest open meetings I ever had was in a working men's club in a mining area in South Yorkshire where there was a tremendous listening to the exposition of the word of God. My experience is that contemporary men and women, even without a biblical background can respond to the proclamation of the truth of the Word of God when the Spirit of God works amongst them. It is still very possible for our gospel to come, as in Paul's day, not only in word but with the Spirit and with power. We are expounding the truth. It is not just that you find Jesus and find something happy, joyful and fulfilling. We dialogue on the truth of Christ's person, his death, his resurrection and his return. We do believe in the lostness of the lost and the awesomeness of eternal damnation. These are things on which we need to dare to speak out. There must be bad news before good news. Evangelism will be basically proclamation-evangelism. That is why I find it difficult to evangelize alongside those who deny the basic truths of the Christian faith. This is the dilemma. This is the pain many of us have. I know it has ever been like that within the Church of England. But it does seem that we move further down that road. How do I evangelize with those who do not believe in the basics of the faith? Compromise on biblical truths will always weaken the message we preach. Ultimately, we are dealing not with peripheral but with central matters, and papering over the cracks will make our credibility less.

The Money Game

I believe the challenge comes in what we do with our

money. The challenge is to the local church and its use of money; all too often this is where it counts. Money must be invested more in mission than in machinery and maintenance, and we need to take a radical look at the stewardship of our resources. I am minister of a very busy parish church on the outskirts of Sheffield and it is right that I challenge my congregation to stewardship. It is equally right that they challenge us as a church to the stewardship of what we do with our money, and unashamedly we invest in gospel ministry. I believe somewhere down the line we need some courage to be radical in that direction. Many people agree that the present system of quota needs urgent overhaul. There must be more liberty and authority for the local church and encouragement to invest in outreach ventures at home and abroad and not be overwhelmed by bureaucratic demands.

Church Planting

We must look at the whole concept of church planting. I think we need to be radical and honest about this. For example, is it right that we should simply live with parish boundaries and assume that every Anglican church is doing its job, when we know deep down in our hearts that not to be so? Have we not some responsibility to seek a gospel ministry in every parish? I come to this Conference from preaching at the institution of a minister in a part of Sheffield. He is not an Anglican but we are twinned with him from our church. There is no gospel ministry in that area, and yes he is crossing somebody else's parish boundary, but I make no apology for that. It seems to me that the gospel is more important than parish etiquette and I believe that at the end of the day we are responsible for the gospel that has been handed down to us. How do we hold it out?

The Best Boat?

I recollect a few years ago a bishop discussing one or two

things with me. He enquired whether I was only an Anglican because I thought it was the best boat to fish out of. I think my slight delay in denying that statement suggested that I did. That is not true, I love the Church of England. I believe the parish system as such has unique opportunities and most of my missioning goes on through local parish churches. I am not sure personally now whether it remains the best boat to fish out of. I think we need to recognize that it is easy in the love and fellowship of meeting one another to have rose-tinted spectacles.

We need to be realistic, and admit that there are very many people who do not listen to what we say because of what they see within the life of the Church of England. I believe we have a tremendous responsibility as evangelicals who are Anglicans. Our concern in *Reform* is that we should not paper over the cracks, that we should not assume that because we can meet together like this we are actually agreed on everything. I believe there are some vital issues where we do differ. Ezekiel talks about the danger of a bulging wall, when you just try to plaster over it and it falls (Ezek. 13.10–16). I hope that at least we will be honest enough to accept these differences. I have come to believe that *Reform* might be seen as a contemporary version of the 'thorn in the flesh' of which Paul speaks in 2 Corinthians 12. Whatever that was in Paul's day, it certainly was used by the Lord to strengthen him and to keep him from triumphalist notions. Perhaps there is still a need for a thorn in the flesh, and certainly we must always, following Paul's testimony in those verses, cease to have reliance on power structures and find our strength in human weakness. Some of us do believe that we have reached days when there is a call for us to risk security in the cause of Christ. I personally have been disturbed frequently over recent months by Hebrews 13.13 and the call to go to Christ 'outside the camp'. I would not pretend to know exactly what that may mean but I do believe the principle remains as vital for evangelical Christians today as it was for those Hebrew Christians so long ago. Sometimes people complain that we have been divisive, that we have been strident. We apologise if that is so. I do not think we have a monopoly of rudeness and stridency, but we are deeply concerned, and I believe that we need all of us to bring ourselves afresh not just under some Anglican evangelical umbrella, but under the word of God.

Under God's Word

We all of us should tremble under the word of God. I am not sure that this is characteristic, as it ought to be, of ourselves as evangelicals today. Do we ourselves understand and can we even begin to communicate to our congregations why it was that the Reformers of 400 years ago were prepared to give their lives for truth and doctrine? Why was it that Cranmer put his hand in the fire because it had written his recantation? I do not believe that we shall be effective in any of our evangelism unless we are faithful under the word of God. It is my privilege to minister in a church where we have a very considerable number of young people, and that age group – which is often missing in churches – is the largest age group in our church. It is for their sake particularly that I believe as evangelical Anglicans we need to be absolutely sure that we put ourselves under God's word, that we do not swerve from it, and that we encourage our evangelical bishops to go on standing firm in that word, for without it we have nothing to offer. I do not think we have much time. I believe there is an urgency, there is an opportunity. God give us grace to be under the word of God, to hold on to it courageously, and hold it out imaginatively.

Notes

1. See chapter 2.
2. Editor's note: This theological position asserts a biblical principle

that only a man should exercise headship (understood as leadership) in marriage, society and church. It is based particularly on the passages which speak of the role of the head in Ephesians 5.22–4, 1 Corinthians 11.3–10 and 1 Timothy 2.11–12.

3. See notes to Chapter 2.

Questions for Discussion

1. Does effective evangelism depend upon consistent evangelicalism?
2. What could be the danger of papering over the cracks of differences among evangelical Anglicans today?
3. Do you believe that the Church of England is still the best boat out of which to fish in evangelism today?

Further Reading

D. M. Lloyd-Jones, *What is an Evangelical?* (Edinburgh, Banner of Truth, 1992).

D. Carson, *A Call to Spiritual Reformation* (Leicester, IVP, 1994).

J. I. Packer, *God has Spoken* (London, Hodder, 1993).

CHAPTER TEN

Stewards of the Spirit

Sandy Millar

I would like to tell you a true story in the hopes that it might encourage us all. A young man called Lee came to our church almost exactly a year ago. He was the Mercury telephone engineer and he was a typical pagan of today, 25-years-old, not believing in anything; he had been in the New Age movement for some time and had flitted from relationship to relationship, different girls all the time. He hankered after spiritual experience, which is what caused him to get involved with the New Age movement. He came to mend the telephone and took an instant liking to our receptionist, for reasons that I entirely understand! He spent most of the morning trying to work out what a proper line for chatting up a church receptionist might be and at lunchtime he went up to her and, with a broad smile, he asked her if it would be possible for her to recommend to him a good Bible. He was very pleased with that as a line! So she recommended a Bible but she also said 'We have a little course that we run [little course! about 600 people now on each Alpha course] when we look at some of the basic ingredients of the Christian faith and we have lots of fun.' In giving his story later he recounted that one of the things that he could not get out of his mind was the juxtaposition of those two things: looking at one or two basic Christian truths and having lots of fun. So he decided that he would join the Alpha Course, which he did, and within about five or six weeks he had given his life to Jesus Christ. At a Sunday evening service about two weeks later he was instantly and totally delivered of a deep, suicidal depression that had had a grip on him for about three years. The Spirit of God came on him and touched him and turned him totally round and he has been growing ever since. In this recent wave of the Holy Spirit, Lee has been on the carpet longer than almost anyone that I know; practically every time the Spirit of God came at the end of a service, there was Lee on the floor and the Spirit of God ministering to him. Here is what he wrote to me at the end of last month:

> I have found that since Toronto [the current move of God's Spirit that has been with us since May 1994] I feel much stronger and able to pray for more people and my prayers for people seem nearly always to be in scriptural terms now. [Bear in mind that he has not been schooled in what would make a theologically acceptable letter.] I am finding I am becoming more disciplined as it were in regards to quiet times and I have a longing for the Word in which the Lord seems to be giving me greater revelation and a longing to pray. My faith is becoming stronger and deeper and I am finding that the more I allow myself to die to self the more freedom and life I am finding in Jesus. I don't know yet how I am to serve the Lord in the years to come, but I have a deep peace and I know that he will make it clear in time.

Supposing for a moment that in order to reach that level of healing and growth in the Spirit of God you had to roar a bit, or moo a bit, or bark a bit, would it not be worth it? I think it would. That is not actually what he has had to do, but I am just assuming the worst case scenario for the moment, because that is what so many tend to assume. So my first point is to draw attention to the astonishing effects all over the country at this time of the Alpha Course. I was asked to tackle the question of 'How are we to reach this country to teach it with the gospel in view of the godlessness of the country and its remoteness from Christ?' I was encouraged to make it personal if I wished. Well, there are now something over 800 Alpha Courses that we know of in this country; they are starting all over the world too: Australia, Canada, New Zealand, the United States, Scandinavia and the rest of Europe. There is even one in Yashka-Ola in the Republic of Mari, some 19 hours east of Moscow by train! I think one reason for this is not just that it is a wonderful course which the Spirit of God has chosen to bless; but because it is based on a number of principles of evangelism that we find working so effectively in the New Testament.

1. Evangelism is most effective through the local church. Here is a quotation from Michael Green which makes the point perfectly: 'We need a thoughtful, sustained, relevant presentation of the Christian faith in work and action, embodied in a warm prayerful lively local church which has a real concern for its community at all levels.[1]
2. Evangelism is a process. Of course you can be converted overnight. But we believe it is more likely to be a process, as birth is a process; a gradual move from unbelief to faith which takes time as things are worked out, questions raised and answered, and the implications taken into account.
3. Evangelism involves the whole person; the head, the heart and the will.
4. Evangelism is integrally related to the supernatural

display of the power of the Holy Spirit. It seems to me to be obvious from the New Testament that the early Church expected to experience and to see the effect of the power of the Holy Spirit in people's lives. They expected to see people healed and changed. They expected to see lives turned upside-down, they expected to experience spiritual gifts and ministries, they expected to see the work of God's Spirit reaching out into every day life. It is the realized experience of the Holy Spirit and it is simply no good telling people that if they understand in their heads they have understood the whole of the Christian faith. So we want to make sure that we have recovered that aspect of church life, the ministry of the Spirit. It is not a modern phenomenon which needs careful controlling, it is an essential ingredient in the New Testament Church which needs developing. In Acts 4 the disciples prayed a twofold prayer; they asked that God would enable his servants to speak his word with great boldness and that God himself would stretch out his hand to heal and perform miraculous signs and wonders through the name of his holy servant Jesus; and he did, and he does! So we need to go on praying for the filling and refilling – that is what makes the evangelism that we are talking about both dynamic and effective and fun.

5. Effective evangelism requires the filling and refilling of the Holy Spirit. The filling of the Holy Spirit is not an option, and if I were to be allowed to make but one serious point today it would be to say that I believe we shall be called to account for our stewardship of this current movement of God's Spirit in this country.

As more and more people come to Christ we must take more seriously the lessons that are to be learned in the area of church planting. I welcome the 'Breaking New Ground' report,[2] but I have to say that it is already being overtaken by events. We must quickly find ways of planting new churches with much more flexibility and speed if a) we are to survive as a denomination and b) we are to respond to what the Spirit of God is doing in our land today. I do not think there has been such an encouraging spiritual climate in the lifetime of any of us previously. It is thrilling! Now is the time; let us go with it; let's go with it together and pray and work to see thousands brought to Christ, in hundreds of new churches, in the next few years.

Notes

1. Michael Green, *Evangelism through the Local Church* (London, Hodder, 1990), preface, p. ix.
2. *Breaking New Ground – Church Planting in the Church of England.* A Report commissioned by the House of Bishops of the General Synod of the Church of England (GS 1099, Church House Publishing, 1994).

Questions for Discussion

1. What physical manifestations do you find described in the Bible that are associated with the appearance of the Spirit of God to people? e.g. falling back, trembling etc?
2. What experience have you of such manifestations today?
3. What plans have you in your church for a basic introductory Christian course?

Further Reading

Patrick Dixon, *Signs of Revival* (Eastbourne, Kingsway, 1994).

Nicky Gumbel, *Questions of Life* (Eastbourne, Kingsway, 1993).

Martin Robinson and Stuart Christine *Planting Tomorrow's Churches Today* (Tunbridge Wells, Monarch, 1992).

CHAPTER ELEVEN

What Should Our Priorities Be?

George Carey

Any form of leadership, as St Peter's Epistle reminds us, is a complex and demanding task. It brings with it great responsibilities – and also great opportunities. Part of our task as leaders, amidst the myriad of calls that demand our attention is to discern what God's priorities are, whether for ourselves or for a parish or for a diocese or for the national Church. It is all too easy to concentrate on secondary issues rather than *the priorities.*

Readers may know this somewhat lengthy letter, written by the Duke of Wellington to the British Foreign Office around the year 1812. It is both clever and sarcastic.

> Gentlemen, while marching from Portugal to a position which commands the approach to Madrid and the French forces, my officers have been diligently complying with your requests which have been sent by His Majesty's ship from London to Lisbon and thence by dispatch rider to our headquarters.
>
> We have enumerated our saddles, bridles, tents

and poles, and all manner of sundry items for which His Majesty's government holds me accountable. I have dispatched reports on the character, wit and spleen of every officer. Each item and every farthing has been accounted for, with two regrettable exceptions for which I beg your indulgence.

Unfortunately, the sum of one shilling and ninepence remains unaccounted for in one infantry battalion's petty cash, and there has been a hideous confusion as to the number of jars of raspberry jam issued to one cavalry regiment during a sandstorm in Western Spain. This reprehensible carelesssness may be related to the pressure of circumstance, since we are at war with France, a fact which may come as a bit of a surprise to you gentlemen in Whitehall.

This brings me to my present purpose, which is to request elucidation of my instructions from His Majesty's government, so that I may better understand why I am dragging an army over these barren plains. I construe that perforce it must be one of two alternative duties, as given below. I shall pursue either one with the best of my ability but I cannot do both:

1) To train an army of uniformed British clerks in Spain for the benefit of the accountants and copy-boys in London, or, perchance,
2) To see to it that the forces of Napoleon are driven out of Spain.

Your Most Obedient Servant,
Wellington

As we focus on our fundamental purpose of proclaiming Christ afresh to our generation, rather than keeping an institution running merely for its own sake, what should our priorities be? Let me suggest four areas which I believe should be commanding our highest attention.

We need to

1. Recover our confidence in the good news which changes lives
2. Refresh our love for God's Church which exists to glorify him
3. Renew our vision for a nation and society which God loves
4. Remain faithful to the charge which we have received.

Recovering our Confidence in the Good News which Changes Lives

Paul's words to the Corinthians: 'I decided to know nothing among you except Jesus Christ and him crucified' (1 Cor. 2.2).

The genius of evangelicalism has always been its consistent emphasis upon the atoning nature of Christ's death on the cross and its power to change lives. It is worth recalling that Paul's theological teaching about the cross went hand in hand with his own personal experience of its reality – of what it had meant for him to turn to Christ and to find new life in him. 'The love of Christ constrains us', he proclaimed (2 Cor. 5.14). It is not only evangelicals who know, share and feel this. It is the heart beat of authentic Christianity from the New Testament onwards; I firmly believe that we shall only recover confidence in the gospel which changes lives when we discover afresh that the cross of Christ is never merely a past event but is always effective in the present. I can say with full integrity that the gospel which called a Dagenham teenager so long ago to follow Christ is still the same exciting one I follow now as Archbishop. There have been hiccups along the way, of course, but the relationship of love and service continues and I am constantly amazed, excited and encouraged by the simplicity and yet the profundity of the good news which has the power to 'ransom, heal, restore and forgive' all who turn to Christ. This is one reason why I am completely committed to this Decade of Evangelism.

One of the important lessons we are learning through the work of 'Food for Thought' and the Springboard team is the way in which those from different traditions in our Church can combine to proclaim the gospel in new and exciting ways. In that team, and in its oversight, the catholic, liberal, evangelical and charismatic traditions merge to work together to bring the good news to a land which needs it so desperately.

One of their cries echoes one of my own. We must find ways of developing a new apologetic for this generation. We cannot rest content and merely repeat the phraseology of a past age. The gospel must be taken to meet the challenges presented to it in the latter part of the twentieth century. We need some of our best minds to combine with those skilled in the art of communication to make this happen. The gospel is not our possession, nor that of any particular group in the Church, but the life giving activity of God in his love for the whole of creation. Like the incarnation itself, in a world in which people get hurt and are destroyed, the gospel has to be earthed in the actual realities of life and related to the culture in which it is proclaimed. This means that we cannot avoid the hard toil that comes from theological exploration as the Church seeks to meet the challenge of modern thought and the explosion of new ideas. Evangelicals must continue to search for excellence in scholarship and an openness to God's truth.

But in talking about a new apologetic I would not wish to confine the task of evangelism to the spoken or written word. Of course, we long for intelligent, effective and Spirit-filled preaching. That should always be our prayer and aim. But proclamation can never be limited to preaching. Like the incarnation, the gospel is most effective when it is embodied by Christians who live the faith in their work-a-day lives and in churches which display its reality. John Finney's book, *Finding Faith Today*, reminds us that more people come to faith through friendship than through large-scale evangelistic events.[1] Living the faith is one of the main ways in which faith will be communicated, and the good news brought to our land.

Refreshing our Love for God's Church which Exists to Glorify Him

At times the Church can be deeply frustrating to belong to, even for Archbishops but, if we are to be true to our calling, then our expressions of extravagant love for Christ's Church should outnumber the criticisms we express. The story is told of a train gently jogging through the Welsh hills. As the gradient increased so the engine got slower and slower. The impatient passenger went up to the front of the train and said to the driver: 'Can't you go any faster?' 'Yes,' said the driver, 'I can go a lot faster but, you see, I have to stay with the train.' Many of us here would love to go faster but we must stay with the train. It is no good if a few get to the top of the hill whilst leaving the vast majority behind!

This is to say what Scripture commands us. To be a member of Christ's Church is not an optional extra, but a central part of our calling. Nor I hope, as Anglicans, will we confine our love either to some mystical idea of the universal Church or to the local congregation we serve. It involves a commitment to churches in community; to the diocese, the national and the world-wide Communion of which we are but a small part.

In these days when we are growing closer together ecumenically, there is always a danger in being heard to sing the praises of a single denomination. Yet there are aspects of Anglicanism that are important gifts to the wider

Church and are therefore something of which we can be proud. For instance, there are our *biblical foundations.* Cranmer, Hooker and many of their contemporaries longed for a Church which conformed to the teachings of Holy Scripture and that of the early Church. That remains the case. Those who believe that Anglicans can believe anything provided that it doesn't make any difference or involve commitment, clearly have not read our Canons or Articles. To be an Anglican is to be earthed in Scripture and taught by the faith of a historic Church or historic Christianity. Let us be in no doubt about that.

Or, again, ours is a Church which has always sought to *encompass variety and differences of outlook, opinion and practice, built on the foundations of the faith once revealed.* Most obviously those have been expressed in the catholic, liberal and evangelical wings of our Church combined with the charismatic but, even within each of those, there has been great variety. I, for one, would have it no other way. One of the things I value increasingly as a member of the Church of England is this diversity. I remain deeply grateful for the Christ-centred faith I was taught as a teenager with its spirituality rooted in Scripture. I hope I shall never depart from those roots. But I have also been enriched by the many treasures I have encountered through experiencing the worship and thinking of other traditions in the wider family of the Church. We would all be much the poorer if we ever tried to constrict that diversity beyond the demands of the gospel itself.

What we see on a small scale in this country is reflected abundantly in the Anglican Communion as a whole. Over the last three years I have had the privilege of seeing something of these differences. I think of the Church in Sabah with its charismatic-evangelical roots, praying and working towards a tenfold increase by the year 2000. Or, south-east from there, in Papua New Guinea, a Church firmly rooted in the catholic tradition making disciples by the score combining faithful teaching and social care, combined with the deployment of hundreds of lay catechists. Across in Tanzania, the Church of that province, nurtured both by CMS and USPG,[2] combines a profound prophetic witness representing the poor and the weak with an uncompromising presentation of the gospel to all. Similarly, in the Church of the Province of Kenya, which owes so much both to CMS and BCMS,[3] their recently-retired Archbishop, Manasses Kuria, will be spending the next few years setting up a project to provide practical help for the street children of Nairobi and to speak to them of Christ at the same time.

Now, none of those Churches is perfect, but they do express the wonderful diversity within Anglicanism. Desmond Tutu's phrase 'the Rainbow people of God' applies equally well to the Church of England and the Anglican Communion, as it does to South Africa. It is something I love and cherish. It is sad when we allow our differences to become a cause for division, often built on ignorance or fear. It is sad when we react and recoil by turning inwards rather than reaching out into the deepening darkness outside us. Although I long for unity with other historic Christian Churches, the breadth, the tolerance, the liturgy, the traditions and the faith of the Anglican Church continue to satisfy me. I invite you, as I do the other great traditions in our Church, to embrace the Church of England as it is; to be committed to its life and to seek to change it so that it conforms more and more to the likeness of the God we serve.

Renewing our vision for a nation and society which God loves

His concern, which must be ours too, is for the whole of humanity and for every aspect of our lives. *Faith in the City* and the Decade of Evangelism are not in conflict; they are all of a piece. Evangelicals of the last century saw this clearly. Wilberforce's great fight against slavery was an expression of his theology of the cross. Shaftesbury's toil on behalf of factory boys and girls, and chimney sweeps, emerged from a compassion which was shaped by his understanding of the love of God. More recently, it has been good to see evangelicals broadening their social and ethical concerns. For evidence of that, look at the subjects being written about in the Grove Booklets on Ethics.[4] I look at the House of Bishops, where some of those most closely involved in issues to do with society come from the evangelical wing. There is a strong tradition here that we can be proud of. We fail the gospel when evangelical witness slides into pietism alone or when it falls away into social justice alone. A fully rounded theology of the kingdom has the cross at its centre and a heart to change the world.

So, I need to ask: Are we renewing our vision for our nation and society? Do we believe that things can be different? As Michael Turnbull, Gavin Reid and others have reminded us, we now live in a missionary situation. Our structures and our thinking must be changed as a result of this. Many in our land simply do not know about Jesus Christ and it is our job to tell his story afresh to our generation. That story needs to be told both by word and through action.

One of my great concerns is that we should redouble our efforts to reach out to the children and young people of our land. Many of them are seeking for spiritual realities and are searching for foundations for their lives. Over the New Year 150,000 young people gathered in Paris for a Taizé Reunion, drawn together by their desire to worship Christ and to work for him. May I contribute to the debate going on at the moment to say that I continue to emphasize the importance of a collective spiritual act at the start of each school day. Over the last few days, Pete Ward, my adviser for youth ministry, has been meeting with others to look at how we can develop Christian youth ministry both in this country and around the world. One thing he and many others are emphasizing is the need to develop worship that is culturally relevant to young people. This is an area where, at present, Anglicans are involved in a number of exciting experiments. It is something we should continue to encourage.

In this missionary situation we cannot afford to be distracted from our primary task. It is right and healthy for our Church that we should encourage widespread and thoughtful debate on a number of specific subjects. For instance, in issuing their report *Issues in Human Sexuality*,[5] the House of Bishops wanted to do precisely that. I hope that many of you will make your own contributions to that debate. However, it would be quite wrong if we allowed that debate to become centred solely on the question of homosexuality and allowed that single issue to dominate the Church's agenda over the next few years. Our priorities must remain the wider ones of sharing the love of God with a needy world and building up the Body of Christ; and it is firmly within those parameters that discussion of such issues should take place.

But, in talking of the missionary nature of the situation facing us, there is a danger of giving the impression that secularism is all-dominant in our society. Most people still have some links to the Church, however tenuous those may be. I am told that one survey suggested that about a quarter of the population of this country will have attended one service or another over the Christmas period. We know 20 million people are baptized Anglicans. Enormous goodwill still exists for the Churches of this land and we in the Church of England have a special responsibility to build on it.

As an Established Church, we have inherited a responsibility to be a guardian of the faith and a repository of valued traditions. I do not intend to revisit the debate which General Synod had in July 1994, but the point was firmly made there that 'establishment' does not equate with privilege but with the responsibility to serve the nation and the many people committed to us.[6] We do so working very fully with our sister Churches in this land and we do so firmly committed to the parochial system which is the heart-beat of the Church of England.

On a broader front, it is encouraging to see that the Church is becoming again a voice that people expect to hear in debates on morality, both public and private. Whilst there is still a long way to go, privatized morality is increasingly being seen for what it always was – a snare in which the sin of selfishness can all too easily have full sway.

In spite, then, of the difficulties we face and the challenges that lie ahead, we can grasp a clear vision and we need not falter in proclaiming God's promises for the days ahead. Two hundred years ago, this country seemed to be heading towards a bleak secular future until men of faith like the Wesley brothers, Charles Simeon and many others took the nation by storm. Are we content to limit our horizons to what we can conceive of as possible, or are we willing to labour and pray for a vision that looks beyond our own survival as a Church to a rejuvenated faith for our people and nation?

Remaining Faithful to the Charge You and I have Received

The Epistle to the Ephesians Chapter 4 begins with these verses:

> I therefore, a prisoner for the Lord, beg you to lead a life worthy of the calling to which you have been called, with all lowliness and meekness, with patience, forbearing one another in love, eager to maintain the unity of the Spirit in the bond of peace.

Here is a call to all Christians, not only to clergy but one that comes especially to us as leaders.

Our calling, as J. C. Ryle, Handley Moule and John Wesley would all want to remind us, is to a life of holiness – to a life that is truly patterned on Christ's. It is that which must govern our thinking and direct our actions. And, as it does so, it will affect the way in which we lead our churches and behave towards our loved ones and families. It will affect the way we seek out the truth, and forbear from judgements based on scant information. It will restrain us from carping criticism and replace that with expressions of true concern and love. It will raise our sights from concentrating overmuch on a few issues and lead us instead to see the world through the eyes of the one who came to save it. It will fire our love for Scripture and compel us to go out and tell our story of the love of God.

And if, like Paul, our response is to cry, 'Who is sufficient for these things?' (2 Cor. 2.16), 'who is sufficient when we are so few and so weak?', may I remind you of that splendid verse in 1 Thessalonians which continues to provide me with guidance and inspiration: 'He who calls you is faithful, and he will do it' (1 Thess. 5.24). Our sufficiency never comes from within ourselves or directives from the House of Bishops or Synod. It is God alone who can equip and sustain us for the good works he has prepared for us. 'He who calls you is faithful and he will do it.' Therefore my brothers and sisters in Christ, let us have a firm resolve to *proclaim Christ afresh to our generation*, secure in the faith to which we have been called, and equipped by the Spirit of God.

Notes

1. John Finney, *Finding Faith Today* (Swindon, British and Foreign Bible Society, 1992).
2. Church Missionary Society and United Society for the Propagation of the Gospel.
3. Bible Churchmens' Missionary Society (now called Crosslinks).

4. Grove Books Ltd., Bramcote, Notts.
5. House of Bishops, *Issues in Human Sexuality* (London, Church House Publishing, 1991).
6. The debate on Direct State Control which was initiated by a Private Member's Motion from Bishop Colin Buchanan (See *Report of Proceedings* July 1994, Vol. 25, No. 2, pp. 303ff).